LOVE
TO
COOK

Tips, techniques and classic recipes

SIMON &
SCHUSTER
ILLUSTRATED

London · New York · Sydney · Toronto · New Delhi

A CBS COMPANY

LOVE TO COOK

Tips, techniques and classic recipes

Waitrose
Cookery School

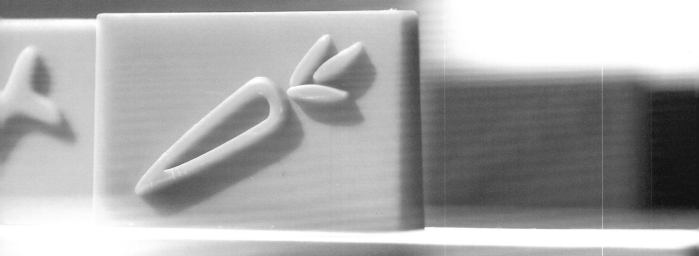

First published in Great Britain in 2011 by Simon & Schuster UK Ltd
A CBS COMPANY

1 3 5 7 9 10 8 6 4 2

SIMON & SCHUSTER ILLUSTRATED BOOKS
Simon & Schuster UK Ltd
222 Gray's Inn Road
London WC1X 8HB

www.simonandschuster.co.uk

Simon & Schuster Australia, Sydney

Simon & Schuster India, New Delhi

A CIP catalogue record for this book is available
from the British Library

ISBN: 978-1-84983-764-4

Editorial director: Francine Lawrence
Project editor: Hilary Ivory
Design: XAB Design
Photography: Ruth Jenkinson
Home economy: Emma Marsden
Production manager: Katherine Thornton
Commercial director: Ami Richards

Printed and bound in the UK by Butler Tanner & Dennis
Colour reproduction by Dot Gradations Ltd, UK

For further information about the Waitrose Cookery School,
visit www.waitrose.com

Few things in life are more important than the food you eat, and a love of good food is at the heart of everything we do at Waitrose. So perhaps it's no surprise that we dreamed for a long time of having a place where we could share our passion for the best ingredients and for cooking. This dream became a reality when, in November 2010, we opened the doors, for the first time, to the Waitrose Cookery School in north London.

Through this book, which is full of recipes and practical tips from the experts who teach at the school, we hope to inspire you to enjoy preparing, cooking, tasting and serving wonderful food to your family and friends. Whether you're already experienced in the kitchen or simply a would-be cook, I hope the pages that follow will motivate you to roll up your sleeves and hit the kitchen!

Mark Price
Managing Director
Waitrose

A shared love of food

"The cornerstone of our philosophy is that cooking is a life skill – at its best, creative, fulfilling and impressive, but also great fun and a good de-stressing mechanism."

Karen Himsworth
General Manager,
Waitrose Cookery School

Sharing a love of cooking with you

If you're a passionate cook, you probably have a repertoire of dishes that's perfect each time. But what if you could give them an added twist? And how about impressing your friends with a three-course meal that could grace the menu of a Michelin-starred venue? Since 2010, our team of professional chefs has taught over 2,000 people to do just that at our state-of-the-art school. Courses range from beginners' basics to the art of Michelin-star cooking. If you've ever experienced the aromatic flavours of a genuine Moroccan tagine, or the perfect combination of lemongrass and coconut in a top Thai restaurant, or you've tried a melt-in-the-mouth pistachio macaron in a Parisian *salon du thé*, you'll find the signature dishes of your favourite cuisines at the cookery school, and also right here in the pages of this book. Because one question everyone who attends inevitably asks is if they can take a chef home to continue the instruction in their own kitchen. This cookbook is our response.

Learning from the experts

Watching TV chefs is daunting, but our chefs love sharing their knowledge. Practice always makes perfect, but learning the tricks of the trade certainly gives confidence. All the chefs at the school have worked their way up through Michelin-starred kitchens - one has even been

awarded a Michelin star in his own right. The cornerstone of our philosophy is that cooking is a life skill: at its best it's creative and impressive, but it's also great fun and a brilliantly effective de-stressing mechanism. Accordingly, both the courses and this book are designed to help, not intimidate, you. Equipment is similar to yours at home - utensils are kept to a minimum, with good quality knives of paramount importance. And if you're unsure about any item, you'll find friendly advice on everything you need to kit out your own kitchen.

Back to school

Once you've acquired the fundamentals, you'll be well on your way to becoming a confident, accomplished cook. The Basic Techniques chapter gives you the same detailed instruction as is taught on our courses that will take your cooking to the next level. And if you can manage to get to the school, you'll be joining like-minded people with a shared thirst for knowledge - because one thing we know is that cooking is a terrific unifier.

We hope you'll experience some of the excitement and passion that we feel about good food in the pages of LOVE TO COOK. We also hope that you'll come and share our love of cooking at the Waitrose Cookery School.

Gordon McDermott
Executive Chef

"I'm totally passionate about food, wine and cooking, and I'm on a mission to pass on my enthusiasm and knowledge."

Eleni Tzirki
Pastry Sous Chef

"My secret ingredient is love – I put a lot of it into my cooking!"

James Campbell
Head Pastry Chef

"The secret is to cook from the heart with ingredients that you love, then the soul and passion will shine through."

Wilson Chung
Sous Chef

"Great food is achievable, so don't be afraid to have a go. Don't put it on a pedestal – put it on a plate."

Gordon came on board to get the cookery school started and to assemble the best team he could find. He brought with him his experience gained at Rick Stein's Padstow Seafood School and Anton Mosimann's Academy. Prior to that, he had cooked for television and in celebrated London restaurants such as Simpson's-in-the-Strand, People's Palace and Quaglino's. His speciality is seafood, but he loves Asian- and oriental-style cooking.

Eleni owes her career, she says, to Regis Beauregard, The Ritz's pastry wizard. After that, she joined Pierre Koffmann at Restaurant On The Roof at Selfridges, before teaming up with Bruno Loubet at The Zetter Hotel's Bistro Bruno.

A member of the Academy of Culinary Arts, James C was Group Head Pastry Chef under Gary Rhodes by the age of 24, then Head Pastry Chef at the Mandarin Oriental, where he cooked for the A-listers.

With a business degree, an early career in media and advertising, and a family background in food, Sydney-born Wilson came to the school after working on *Ready Steady Cook* and *MasterChef*, Australia.

James Bennington
Head Chef

"Good food doesn't have to be complicated – simple things are often the best."

Claire Lanza
Chef Trainer

"My dad is Italian, so I was born to love food and cooking !"

Jon Jones
Chef Trainer

"Nothing beats the pride I feel from seeing people tuck into food that I've prepared from start to finish."

Awa Jammeh
Chef Assistant

"I really enjoy the happy atmosphere of the cookery school and the inspirational chefs."

Before joining the school, James' career spanned London's Chez Bruce and two-Michelin-starred The Square. But it was as Head Chef at London's La Trompette that he gained a Michelin star in his own right.

With a degree in Modern Languages and a Leith's Diploma in Food & Wine, Claire was Gary Rhodes' sous chef for his TV series, *Rhodes Across Italy*. She has also been a private chef and worked in the wine trade.

A graduate of the three-year Specialised Chef Scholarship at Bournemouth College, Jon worked at Langan's Brasserie and also as Junior Sous Chef at Fortnum & Mason and Whitechapel Dining Room (two rosettes).

Swedish-born and of Gambian heritage, Awa has a background in restaurants and retail. Cooking is a big part of her life, and she often cooks the school's recipes at home for friends and family.

"If you're serious about producing great results in the kitchen, there's no doubt that it's made a whole lot easier when you have the right kit."

equipment

Metal Tongs
Good idea for turning
meat, fish and poultry

Fish Slice
Useful for flipping and
removing delicate
pieces of fish

Ladle, Medium
For serving sauces

Measuring Spoons
Gives accurate
measurements for
all baking needs

All-Clad Serving Spoon
For dishing up food such
as creamy mashed potato

Chinois
For straining sauces
and soups to achieve
a smooth finish

All-Clad Slotted Serving Spoon
Makes removing vegetables from
boiling water easy

"Invest in good-quality basics before anything else — first-class, durable cookware will pay dividends over the years."

Small Colander
For straining foods with liquids such as pasta or potatoes

All-Clad Saucepan, Small with Lid
Perfect for poaching and making sauces

Mermaid Baking Trays
Nonstick trays perfect for cooking roast potatoes

Le Creuset Casserole
Available in several colours - brilliant way to do casseroles and stews

Le Creuset Cast Iron Grill Pan
This gets extremely hot, providing a delicious chargrilled finish to meat, poultry and vegetables

All-Clad Saucepan, Large with Lid
Good for stews

Cooling Rack
Allows bread and cakes to cool quickly, ensuring they can breathe without sweating

All-Clad Nonstick Frying Pan
Good for frying fish – gives a nice crispy skin

All-Clad Stainless Steel Frying Pan
Works well for frying, as it holds the heat very well

Steamer Petal
Very handy alternative to an electric streamer - place in a wok or pan with a little water

Le Creuset Tagine
Its shape retains the delicate flavours of a meat or fish tagine

All-Clad Wok with Lid
Very useful for quick stir-fries

"Consider the gadgets that will reduce hassle, give polished results and turn the kitchen into an oasis of calm."

Joseph Joseph Chopping Boards
Colour-coded for easy kitchen use and storage

Whisk
For whisking small amounts of cream or egg whites

Kenwood Food Processor
Great for making pasta dough or crushed ice for cocktails

Kenwood kMix Hand Blender
Turns cabbage into coleslaw, makes soup light and frothy, and ganache smoothly silky

Rolling Pin (plastic)
For rolling pastry and pounding spices

OXO Speed Peeler
Peels vegetables in a flash

Kenwood Hand Mixer
Designed for everyday use, such as whipping cream in a flash

Lock & Lock Storage Containers
Clear plastic and leak-proof, the best way to store food and lock in smells, keeping your fridge tidy and fragrant

Potato Ricer
For exquisite, lump-free mashed potato

Pestle and Mortar
For crushing spices or pounding garlic

Spatula
Scrapes out bowls thoroughly and efficiently

OXO Good Grips Mandolin Slicer
Very sharp blade that enables very fine slicing

Kenwood kMix Mixing Bowl
Funky colours to fit any kitchen. Make sure you start on a low speed and increase gradually - perfect for light, fluffy meringues

Wooden Spoons
For stirring sauces and risottos in non-scratch pots

OXO Good Grips Box Grater
A sturdy grater for cheese and zesting fruit

Pyrex Jugs and Bowls
Excellent for mixing, storing and measuring

Robert Welch Knife Block
The built-in ceramic sharpening wheel means you can maintain a razor-sharp edge to your knife

Tala Digital Timer
Vital piece of kit to keep you on track

Imperia Pasta Machine
Rolls out perfect dough for ravioli, tagliatelle or pappardelle

Pastry Brush (wooden)
For brushing raw dough to create a golden, crisp finish

Pastry Cutters
For cutting out biscuit shapes

Basic techniques 1

Knife skills

We've all tried, at one time or another, to do something fiddly without the right tools. Sure, you can hack away at a fish or a mango with a bread knife, but it won't be a pretty sight. There are reasons why food emerges from a professional kitchen looking as it does, and one is that chefs use the right tools for the task. The knives on this page will help you achieve the right results - just remember, you need to keep your knives sharp.

Before you buy

Pick up the knife and test the weight in your hand. Make sure it fits and feels comfortable when you apply downward pressure, as when you're cutting, chopping and slicing.

Before you start chopping, wet a clean J-cloth or piece of kitchen towel and lay it flat on a work surface, then place your chopping board on top of it. That will prevent it from slipping and causing a potentially nasty accident.

Carving knife Before carving meat, let it rest for 10 minutes. Don't force the knife - use a long, slow slicing motion from top to bottom. **Leg of lamb** Carve towards the leg. **Pork** Remove crackling and set aside, then slice thickly, top to bottom. **Roast chicken** Remove the breasts, then drumsticks, and cut in half; then slice the breast and serve, keeping the bones for stock. **Roast beef** Slice against the grain.

Cook's knife When chopping an onion, remove the point, cut in half through the root and peel off the skin. Slice across vertically from the root (use its natural lines to guide you). Don't cut the whole way through - you want the root to hold the end of it together while you cut. Now cut a horizontal slice halfway up the onion about an inch away from the root, as in the picture, and start slicing across to produce little pieces.

Prep knife This small knife is ideal for intricate work: it's easy to handle and the small blade allows you to cut around and through ingredients such as fruit and vegetables. It has a serrated edge and a small blade designed to cut away peel without losing too much of the fruit underneath.

Fish-filleting knife No other knife will do quite as good a job of filleting fish as a proper fish knife. The blade is smaller, finer and more flexible than any other, enabling it to get in between the delicate flesh and the small bones in order to separate them.

Boning knife This knife is rigid, has a curved tip and a far stronger blade in order to cope with the tough job of getting through meat fibres and around bones.

How to fillet
a round fish

This method is the most effective and also the technically correct way to fillet sea bass, mackerel, trout, sea bream, John Dory, cod, pollock, coley, mullet, black bream and sardines. You'll need a pair of scissors and a sharp fish knife. It has a flexible blade that allows you to work your way easily between the flesh of the fish and the delicate bones.

To make fish stock

Remove the head from the fish and discard. Put the bones into a medium saucepan and add 1 chopped leek, 1 celery stick, 1 small onion, 1 fresh bay leaf and 1 litre cold water, and bring to the boil. Skim and discard the froth from the top, turn down to a medium heat and simmer for 15 minutes. Strain and freeze until you need to use it.

Put the fish on a board and, using a pair of scissors, trim off the gills on either side of the fish and any that run along the top of it.

With the point of a sharp knife, pierce the stomach of the fish about 2.5cm from the tail and run the knife from tail to head until the knife naturally stops. Using your fingers, clean the insides and run the stomach cavity under a cold tap for 30 seconds.

Place the fish on a chopping board and make a sweeping cut around the head on both sides. This should follow the shape of the fish and run just below the gills.

With the head facing away from you and spine towards the knife hand, start at the head and run the knife along the top of the spine to the tail in a gentle slicing - not sawing - action, with the blade working between the spine and the flesh to remove the fillet. Repeat until the fillet begins to come away. From time to time, lift the fillet to check where you're working.

When you get to the rib bones, let the knife follow the shape of the fish and slice through. Once you've removed the fillet, set it aside.

Turn over the fish and repeat with the second fillet, this time starting at the tail and working towards the head. Be careful - the second fillet may be a little trickier. Now you have two fillets ready to cook.

How to fillet
a flat fish

This method is the most useful way to get to grips with filleting lemon sole, plaice, brill, halibut, turbot, Dover sole, witch sole or any other flat fish. Just make sure your knife is really sharp before you start.

For a simple and delicious fish stock recipe, see page 25.

Place the fish flat on a chopping board and, using a pair of scissors, trim off the small fins. With a sharp knife, cut a semi-circle around the head just under the gills. (Or, if you prefer, you can use a strong, sharp pair of scissors to completely remove the head.)

Make an incision from the head to the tail, straight along the centre of the fish. You'll feel the knife stop as it hits the bone. Use a long, slicing action - don't chop.

Now you're ready to start removing the top two fillets. Following the line you've made down the centre of the fish, start to slice away under the fillet, following the contours of the tiny bones. Continue until you come to the outer fins and then remove the fillet.

To make it easier, now turn the fish with the tail facing way from you and repeat Step 3. (Sometimes you'll get a large piece of roe under this fillet.)

Turn the fish over and make the same incision around the top of the head and repeat the cut down the centre of the fish. This side can be easier, as you'll have a line to follow from head to tail. Again, start to remove the fillet from the bone.

Repeat the previous steps by removing the fourth fillet. Remember, filleting the bottom side of the fish may be a little more difficult, as you'll have lost the support given by the top two fillets.

How to joint a chicken

Knowing how to joint a chicken is the best way of getting the most from a whole bird. Use the leftover bones to make stock (see right). Equip yourself with a sharp boning knife, which will allow you to carve easily between the bones and the flesh.

To make chicken stock

1 Place the leftover bits in a pan with 6 black peppercorns, 1 bay leaf, 1 chopped onion, 1 carrot, 2 celery sticks and 2 litres cold water.

2 Bring to the boil and skim off any impurities. Simmer for 1 hour.

3 Strain into a sealable container and keep refrigerated for up to 3 days, or freeze for up to 1 month.

4 For a more intensely flavoured stock, after straining, simmer until reduced by half.

Place the bird breast side up on the chopping board with the cavity facing away from you. Pull the leg away from the body, making the skin taught. Using the blade of the knife, not the tip, cut through the skin between the breast and the leg.

Bend the leg out and away from the body and down towards the chopping board. You will hear a 'click' as you release the leg from its socket. Cut through the ball joint to release it completely, keeping as much of the leg meat intact as possible. Repeat for the other leg.

Place the bird breast side up on the chopping board with the cavity facing away from you. Feel along the breastbone to check where to insert the knife. Working slightly to the left of the breastbone, cut along its length from top to bottom.

Cut cleanly between the breast meat and the breastbone using the natural line of the breast-bone as a guide. Your knife should always be in contact with the breastbone to ensure that you get as much flesh off the bone as possible. Cut through the ball joint to release the breast from the carcass, leaving the wing attached to the breast. Cut off the wing tips.

Place the legs skin side down on the chopping board. Locate the ball joint between the thigh and drumstick. Cut through the ball joint cleanly to separate the two pieces of meat. Repeat for the other leg.

Place the two breasts on the chopping board skin side up. Cut the breast into two pieces by cutting through the meat at an angle towards the wing. Repeat for the other breast. You now have 8 equal pieces of chicken - 4 pieces of brown meat and 4 pieces of white meat.

How to make fresh pasta

Sure, you can buy pasta - including fresh pasta - from the chill cabinet. But nothing beats the look of awe and admiration on the faces of friends and family than when you serve up pasta you have made yourself. It's simpler than you think and it elevates a humble bowl of pasta to something approaching an art form.

Serves 2 **Prepare** 1 hour, plus 45 minutes kneading and resting, depending on the recipe you're making. (See page 137 for how to apply this technique to Spinach & Ricotta Tortellini.)
Cook 3-4 minutes

(See page 137 for how to apply this technique to Spinach & Ricotta Tortellini.)

You will need

95g 00 pasta flour, sieved, plus extra for dusting
1 large egg
1 egg yolk

Put the flour on to a clean, dry work surface and make a well in the centre.

Crack the egg and yolk into the middle and then, using your fingers, mix the eggs together and start to work them into the flour until you have a firm dough. Knead for 10 minutes until the dough becomes smooth, soft and supple, but not sticky.

Wrap the dough in cling film and allow it to rest for 20 minutes in a cool place.

Cut the dough in half. With a rolling pin, roll out the pasta to a thickness of 1cm. Now pass the dough through the widest setting of the pasta machine.

Fold each end of the length of pasta in on itself to create a 'book turn'. Roll the pasta again through the widest setting. Repeat the process of book turning and re-rolling three times. These book turns help create strength in the pasta and give it a silky texture.

Roll the pasta through the machine, starting with the thickest gauge, until you reach the narrowest. It gets longer as it gets thinner, so shout for help if needs be. Cut it thinly to make spaghetti or thickly to make tagliatelle. Place on a tray dusted with pasta flour for 30 minutes to dry out. Or use it to make tortellini (see recipe on page 137).

How to make sweet pastry

Sweet or short pastry is one of the fundamentally great things any keen cook should have in their repertoire. This recipe uses the creaming method, as it allows the pastry to become more elastic and, therefore, more user-friendly.

Makes enough for 1 large (30cm) tart or 6 individual (8cm) tarts
Prepare 45 minutes **Cook** 1 hour, including resting time

You will need

135g unsalted butter, diced
90g caster sugar
1 large egg
270g plain flour
Pinch salt

Put the butter in a bowl with the caster sugar and beat together using a wooden spoon. You don't want the mixture to be too fluffy, so beat it just enough to bring it together.

Add the egg to the mixture and beat. You can use an electric beater for this.

Add a pinch of salt to the flour. Once the egg has been incorporated, start to add the flour gradually in three separate batches, making sure you combine all the butter that's sticking to the bowl, too.

Turn the pastry out on to a lightly floured work surface and knead gently and quickly until it all comes together. You need a light touch here – if you work it too much or too heavily the pastry will become too short once cooked.

Wrap the pastry in some cling film and chill for 30 minutes. This is essential, because not only will it make the pastry easier to work with, it will allow it to rest, which helps to prevent it shrinking in the tin while it's being baked.

Remove from the fridge and unwrap. Place on a lightly floured work surface, roll and shape to the thickness and size you require.

How to make spring onion mash

To make the smoothest mash in the world you need a ricer. Using one guarantees that your mash will be totally lump-free, and that's a promise. This recipe gives a really luxurious texture - smooth, creamy and melt-in-the-mouth.

Serves 4 **Prepare** 20 minutes **Cook** 30 minutes

You will need

1kg Maris Piper potatoes
1 tsp fine table salt
1 bunch spring onions, finely sliced, keeping the green separate from the white
200ml whipping cream
100ml whole milk
100g unsalted butter
Large pinch ground white pepper

Peel the potatoes and cut in half.

Add to a large pot and cover generously with cold water. Season with ½ tsp of the salt and bring to the boil. Simmer for 20 minutes.

While the potatoes are cooking, put the white of the spring onions, cream, milk and butter in a small pan and gently warm until the butter has fully melted. Don't allow it to boil, or this will spoil the milk.

When the potatoes are cooked (check this by piercing a potato or two with a sharp knife) strain the water through a colander into the sink, then cover the pot containing the potatoes with a tea towel or a clean J-cloth (without a lid), and allow them to steam-dry for 3-5 minutes.

Mash the potatoes by putting a couple at a time into the ricer and squeezing them through, allowing the mash that emerges from the other side to fall back into the pot.

Pour the warm cream and milk mixture, chopped green spring onion, remaining ½ tsp salt and white pepper into the mashed potato, and mix through. Beat until smooth and creamy. Serve piping hot.

How to make amazing chips

Is there anything as comforting as hot, lightly salted chips? They've been giving pleasure all over the Western world for around 150 years. These are triple-cooked, which may seem a bit over the top, but it gives the best results - crispy golden on the outside and soft and inviting inside. If your deep-fat fryer isn't big enough to cook all the potatoes at once, do them in batches to avoid overloading the fryer, which will produce soggy chips.

Serves 2 **Prepare** 15 minutes **Cook** 40 minutes, approx.

You will need

Maris Piper potatoes, peeled
1 litre vegetable oil for deep-frying
Large pinch coarse sea salt for
  seasoning

Semi-prepare up to one day in advance. Cover and chill the chips at the end of Step 5, then complete Step 6 the next day. Serve hot!

Bring a large pan of water to the boil (but don't salt the water!). Preheat a deep-fat fryer to 140°C. Cut the potatoes into chunky chips measuring about 2cm x 5cm.

Cook the chips in boiling water until they are soft, but still whole. This is the first 'cooking'.

Once cooked, remove the chips from the water, drain on an absorbent cloth (as above), and allow the chips to steam-dry under a tea towel until cool.

Add the chips to the oil and cook until they are lightly golden brown with a crust on the outside - this will take about 5 minutes.

Remove from the oil and drain on an absorbent cloth. This is the second 'cooking'.

Increase the temperature of the fryer to 190°C. Repeat the frying process in the hotter oil until the chips are crisp and a deeper golden brown. This is the third 'cooking'. Remove, drain and season with a little sea salt. Serve hot.

How to make crème anglaise

Crème anglaise (or 'fresh custard') is without doubt the most versatile and luxurious sauce. This particular recipe also works brilliantly as a base for ice cream, and it's a lot easier than you think. Once the custard is chilled, transfer the mixture to an ice-cream machine and churn until firm, then freeze. Alternatively, leave out the vanilla and use any other flavouring that takes your fancy.

You will need

½ vanilla pod, halved
125ml double cream
125ml whole milk
3 medium egg yolks
50g caster sugar

Serves 4-6 **Prepare** 10 minutes **Cook** 10 minutes

Take the vanilla pod and use the tip of a knife to scrape along the split pod, removing the seeds.

Pour the cream and milk into a small pan, add the vanilla seeds and pod, and bring gently to the boil.

Meanwhile, place the egg yolks and caster sugar in a large bowl and, using a whisk, beat together until pale.

Once the cream mixture has come to the boil, pour over the yolk mixture, whisking constantly.

Transfer the combined mixtures back to the pan and cook over a very low heat, stirring constantly to avoid the eggs scrambling.

Continue this process until the consistency of the custard coats the back of a spoon, then transfer immediately to a bowl and cool as quickly as possible (sitting it over a bowl of iced water is the most effective way). Cover and refrigerate once cooled and serve when required, or within 3 days.

10 classic
sauces

Green peppercorn sauce

Green peppercorns (as opposed to pungent black or red ones) have a fresh, piquant flavour and a bright aroma, which makes this sauce work well with grilled meats and chicken. *Photographed in the jug.*

Serves 4

2 tbsp vegetable oil
2 large banana shallots, finely diced
2 garlic cloves, finely chopped
Salt
2 tbsp green peppercorns in brine, drained
4 tbsp brandy
400ml beef stock
200ml whipping cream
4 tsp Dijon mustard

Prepare 5 minutes
Cook 10-15 minutes

1 Heat the oil in a medium-sized saucepan over a medium heat and cook the shallots and garlic with a pinch of salt until lightly browned and softened. This will take about 5-10 minutes.

2 Add the peppercorns and fry for a further 2 minutes, then add the brandy and cook to reduce to a glaze.

3 Pour the stock into the pan, bring to the boil then stir in the cream and mustard. Bring back to the boil and cook until reduced to a light coating consistency.

4 Season to taste, then serve straightaway.

Béarnaise sauce

This buttery sauce is closely related to hollandaise, except that it also has fresh tarragon and shallots - a great companion for meat and fish. *Photographed in the bowl.*

Serves 4

½ medium-sized shallot, finely chopped
60ml dry white wine
40ml white wine vinegar
2 medium egg yolks
Salt
150g unsalted butter, melted
4-5 sprigs fresh tarragon, finely chopped

Prepare 20 minutes
Cook 15 minutes

1 Place the shallot, wine and vinegar in a saucepan and bring to the boil. Cook until reduced by half. Allow to cool slightly.

2 Pour the reduction into a bowl and add the egg yolks with a pinch of salt. Place the bowl over a pan of barely simmering water, making sure the base doesn't touch the water.

3 Whisk the egg yolks and reduction together continuously over the simmering water until it doubles in volume (about 3-4 minutes). The mixture is ready when it holds the shape of a figure of 8.

4 Remove the bowl from the heat and gradually add the warm, melted butter to the mixture, whisking in a little at a time.

5 When ready to serve, stir in the chopped tarragon.

Caramelised onion gravy

A sauce that was born to be served with Toad in the Hole (see page 175): the sweet onions really complement the crispy batter and juicy sausages.

Serves 4

25g butter
1 tbsp vegetable oil
2 large onions, finely sliced
Pinch sugar
200ml Madeira
1 tbsp flour
500ml beef stock
Salt and freshly ground black pepper

Prepare 10 minutes
Cook 50-55 minutes

1 Melt the butter in a medium-sized saucepan with the oil. When the butter stops foaming, add the onions and sugar. Cook over a medium heat for 20-30 minutes until the onions begin to caramelise.

2 Now pour the Madeira into the pan. Bring to the boil, stirring all the time to deglaze the pan. This allows the caramelised deliciousness on the bottom of the pan to dissolve into the Madeira, enriching the finished sauce. Continue to cook gently for 5 minutes or until reduced by half.

3 Add the flour and cook over a low heat for 2 minutes, stirring constantly.

4 Pour in the stock, stirring all the time with a whisk. Bring to the boil and simmer gently over a low heat for 20 minutes, or until the sauce reaches a light coating consistency. If you like it smoother, blend it in a liquidiser. Season to taste and serve.

Chimichurri sauce

This green sauce is a great steak marinade from Argentina and Uruguay. Our favourite story about its origins is that it's a corruption of 'Jimmy McCurry', an Irishman who supported Argentine independence and marched with General Belgrano's troops in the 19th century, who was reputedly the first person to make it. Whatever the truth, it's utterly delicious.

Serves 4

½ large red chilli, halved, deseeded and finely chopped
6 garlic cloves, peeled and finely grated
Small bunch fresh flat-leaf parsley (leaves only), finely chopped
4 heaped tsp dried oregano
1 tsp sea salt flakes
5 tbsp red wine vinegar
4 tbsp extra virgin olive oil

Prepare 20 minutes

Combine all the ingredients in a large bowl with 5 tbsp cold water, mixing them together well. Chill in the fridge until required.

Chipotle chilli ketchup

More than a ketchup, this is almost a gourmet dipping sauce. The combination of fiery, smoky chipotle chillies with wine vinegar, brown sugar and strong Worcestershire sauce goes with just about anything.

Serves 8

4 tbsp sunflower oil
1 medium onion, finely chopped
1 bay leaf, stalk removed and finely chopped
1 sprig thyme, leaves picked
2½ tsp chipotle chilli paste
½ tsp ground coriander
½ tsp ground cumin
600ml passata
4 tbsp red wine vinegar
2 tbsp light brown sugar
½ tsp clear honey
2 tsp Worcestershire sauce

Prepare 30 minutes
Cook 40 minutes

1 Heat the oil in a heavy-based pan. Add the onion and fry over a medium heat for 12 minutes or until the onion is golden and translucent.

2 Add the bay leaf, thyme and chilli paste and stir through.

3 Add the coriander, cumin, passata, vinegar and sugar and bring to the boil. Simmer on a medium heat for 20 minutes until the mixture begins to thicken.

4 When the mixture is thick, add the honey and Worcestershire sauce. Bring to the boil again then take off the heat. Pour into a sterilised Kilner jar and cool. Store in the fridge and use within 3 weeks.

Salsa verde

Italian for 'green sauce', it's usually eaten cold as a dipping sauce for meat, poultry, fish or vegetables - in other words, this sauce also goes with literally anything!

Serves 4-6

Small bunch fresh flat-leaf parsley
Small bunch fresh mint
Small bunch fresh basil
1 garlic clove
1 tbsp Dijon mustard
1 tbsp salted capers, rinsed
4 anchovy fillets in oil, drained
4 tbsp extra virgin olive oil
2 tbsp lemon juice

Prepare 10 minutes

1 Strip the leaves from the herbs and place in a food processor with all the other ingredients.

2 Blitz to a coarse sauce (don't make it too smooth). Scrape the sides of the blender occasionally to make sure all the ingredients have been mixed together. Alternatively, chop the dry ingredients by hand before mixing with the oil and lemon juice to give a lovely, chunky texture.

Lemon aïoli

This is the perfect partner for seafood, poultry or vegetables.

Serves 4

1 large egg yolk
1 tsp lemon juice
1 tsp Dijon mustard
3 garlic cloves, crushed
Salt
225ml groundnut oil
100ml extra virgin olive oil

Prepare 15 minutes

1 Whisk together the egg yolk, lemon juice, mustard, garlic and a little salt in a medium-sized bowl.

2 Very gradually whisk in the groundnut oil and olive oil. At first, add just a few drops at a time, then, once an emulsion forms, pour in a more generous stream. Halfway through whisking, once the mayonnaise seems too thick to continue, stop adding the oil.

3 Cover and chill, bringing it back to room temperature before serving. This will keep in the fridge for 3 days.

Tomato sauce

Can there be anything simpler than homemade tomato sauce? It captures all the vibrant, sunny flavours of Italy and, while it's great as a basic sauce for pasta, it's also a terrific substitute for bottled ketchups which you can add as a condiment to whatever you like.

Serves 4

6 tbsp extra virgin olive oil
1 garlic clove, finely chopped
400g can chopped tomatoes
Sprig basil leaves
Salt and freshly ground black pepper

Prepare 15 minutes
Cook 35 minutes

1 Heat the oil in a medium pan over a low heat and cook the garlic for around 2 minutes without colouring, or until soft.

2 Add the tomatoes, basil and salt and pepper to taste and cook on a medium heat for about 20 minutes, stirring occasionally until thickened. If you don't plan to use this right away, cool it and keep in the fridge.

Sweet chilli dipping sauce

This has so many potential uses that it's impossible to list them all: spring rolls, barbecued meats and chicken, fish 'n' chips - whatever you'd eat with tomato sauce will generally go well with sweet chilli sauce, too.

Serves 4

1 garlic clove, finely chopped
1 large red chilli, finely chopped (seeds optional)
50g caster sugar
3 tbsp white wine vinegar

Prepare 15 minutes
Cook 10-15 minutes

1 Place the garlic, chilli, sugar and vinegar together in a small pan and add 100ml water.

2 Bring to the boil and simmer for 3-5 minutes until the chilli is soft and the sauce is reduced by half, or has a syrup consistency.

3 Remove from the heat, then pour into a small dish and leave to cool.

Chocolate sauce

No need to say anything more about this sauce. Chocolate heaven!

Serves 4

150ml whipping cream
75g bitter chocolate, broken into pieces
25g milk chocolate, broken into pieces

Prepare 5 minutes
Cook 5 minutes

Bring the cream to the boil in a saucepan. Remove from the heat, and whisk in the chocolate until melted. Pour into a jug and serve.

How to present food

Presenting food exquisite enough to be photographed isn't hard once you know how. Here's how the professionals create a pleasing visual structure when the dish involves several disparate elements. Lay out the plates (make sure they're warm if the dish is hot). How many components are there? Vegetables? Sauces? Garnish? The secret lies in positioning one element at a time on each of the plates in one go before moving on to plate up the next (called 'military style', for obvious reasons). Here's how.

To cook this dish...

Turn to page 78 for the recipe for Herb-crusted Veal with Polenta Fries, Olive Purée & Sauce Vierge as seen here. It's a classic example of fine dining.

Work from the centre of the plate outwards. Start by creating a frame - we've done this using the tapenade. A good visual trick is to work in odd numbers, as this balances the component that's in the middle (here it'll be the veal). So: 3 dabs of tapenade, 3 or 5 polenta chips, 9 pieces of tomato.

Once you've created your tapenade frame, place the component that forms the focal point of the plate at the centre - the juicy veal topped with a crust.

Now add the next set of components - the polenta chips. You'll need to have all your cooked ingredients to hand and then move quite quickly to avoid the food getting cold.

Continue building the dish using the artichokes, but be careful not to overload the plate. Serve any extra ingredients, such as the polenta chips or dressing, in separate bowls for your guests to help themselves to more if they wish.

Now for the sauce or dressing. Don't add it any earlier, as it could end up looking dry or congealed, or run on to the rim of the plate. Here, we gently spoon over the chunky sauce vierge. In a restaurant, even though this is a dressing, each visible ingredient would be carefully placed to fall on a chip or lean on the veal to create clean lines.

Lastly, add anything that may collapse, soften or wilt when combined with heat - here, it's the aromatic basil and shavings of Parmesan. Carefully wipe any smears off the plates, and quickly serve.

Simple suppers 2

Tomato-crusted rack of lamb with baby vegetables

There's something spring-like and optimistic about this dish. Although the recipe calls for carrots and courgettes, feel free to use any other baby vegetables that are in season, and take advantage of spring lamb when it's available.

Serves 4

400g baby new potatoes, halved
400g baby carrots, scrubbed
400g baby courgettes, roughly chopped
20-24 Kalamata olives, pitted
Finely grated zest and juice of 1 lemon
2 tsp caster sugar
4 tbsp olive oil
Salt and freshly ground black pepper
1 lean rack of lamb, fat trimmed off
4 tbsp sundried tomato paste
Small bunch fresh flat-leaf parsley, chopped

Prepare 10 minutes
Cook 30-40 minutes

1 Preheat the oven to 220°C/200°C fan oven/gas mark 7. Toss the potatoes, carrots and courgettes in a roasting tin with the olives, lemon zest and juice, sugar and olive oil. Season well and cook in the oven for 15 minutes until just tender. Remove from the oven and stir to turn the vegetables.

2 Put the lamb on a board and spread the tomato paste over the meat. Place on top of the vegetables. Return to the oven and roast for 12-15 minutes for medium; allow an extra 5-8 minutes if you prefer the lamb well done, covering it loosely with foil if it begins to burn.

3 Remove from the oven and allow the lamb to rest on a separate plate for 5 minutes. Stir the chopped parsley and a little extra lemon juice into the vegetables, then divide between two plates.

4 Cut the lamb into cutlets, arrange on top of the vegetables and serve immediately.

> **Wine suggestion**
> Try wines based on Tempranillo or Grenache - their juicy, intense flavours will complement the depth of the sundried tomato and the tender texture of the lamb.

"Try swapping the lamb with monkfish, and marinate in exactly the same way." **Jon's tip**

52

Simple suppers

Oregano marinated lamb with fruity rice

Wherever apricots are combined with lamb and rice, we think of the Middle East or North Africa. But the unusual aspect of this dish is that the apricots are actually cooked in the rice, giving an element of rich sweetness.

Serves 4

2 tbsp olive oil
Grated zest and juice of 1 lemon
4 sprigs fresh oregano, leaves
    only, roughly chopped
Salt and freshly ground black pepper
4 lamb leg steaks or rumps
225g long grain rice
1 cinnamon stick
1 star anise
1 bay leaf
100g soft apricots, roughly chopped
600ml vegetable stock
2 tbsp pine nuts, toasted
Small bunch fresh coriander, roughly
    chopped

Prepare 20 minutes, plus 15 minutes
    marinating
Cook 40 minutes

1 Put the olive oil, lemon zest and juice, oregano and a little seasoning together in a wide, shallow, non-metallic bowl, then use a fork to whisk together. Add the lamb and turn to coat in the marinade. Cover and chill for 15 minutes.

2 Meanwhile, place the rice in a saucepan with the cinnamon stick, star anise, bay leaf, apricots and a pinch of salt, then pour in the vegetable stock and bring to the boil. Cover and simmer over a low heat for 15-20 minutes, until all the liquid has been absorbed and the rice is tender.

3 About 10 minutes before the rice is ready, heat a large frying pan until hot and add the lamb, reserving the marinade. Cook for 3-4 minutes on each side for medium-cooked meat. Add the marinade and cook for 1 minute more, then remove the pan from the heat.

4 Remove the cinnamon stick, star anise and bay leaf from the pan of cooked rice and discard, then stir in the pine nuts and coriander. Divide the rice between four plates, top with the lamb, and serve with the hot juices spooned over.

Pan-fried prawns with mango salsa

This Thai-inspired dish is incredibly quick and easy, and the fresh prawns, leaves and mango make it healthy, too. Assemble the mango salad, then call everyone to the table. By the time they're seated, the prawns and garlic will be cooked and the meal will be ready to serve.

Serves 4

2 tbsp olive oil
2 garlic cloves, finely chopped
400g peeled raw tiger prawns, de-veined
250g soft salad leaves, such as mixed baby leaf and rocket

For the mango salsa:

2 ripe mangoes, peeled, stoned and roughly chopped
2 large red chillies, halved, deseeded and finely chopped
Small bunch mint, roughly chopped
4 spring onions, finely sliced
Juice of 2 limes
1 tsp caster sugar
1 tsp Thai fish sauce

Prepare 30 minutes, plus marinating
Cook 10 minutes

1 To make the salsa, place the mango in a bowl together with the chilli, mint, spring onions, lime juice, sugar and fish sauce. Season to taste, then cover and set aside for 5 minutes to allow the flavours to infuse.

2 Heat the oil in a frying pan and add the garlic. Cook for 10 seconds, then add the prawns and cook for a further 2-3 minutes, turning occasionally until pink and cooked through, ensuring the garlic doesn't burn.

3 Toss the prawns and pan juices with the salad leaves. Divide the mango salsa between two plates and serve the prawns on top.

"Add some papaya and pomegranate seeds to the salad to give it extra flavour and texture." **Jon's tip**

Bacon & artichoke pasta

The artichoke is one of the unsung heroes of the cookery school – we use it a lot, but feel it never gets the recognition it deserves. Here, it's beautifully prepared with salty bacon, sundried tomatoes and chilli, and it works well with pasta shapes other than spaghetti, too.

Serves 4

400g dried spaghetti
280g jar grilled artichokes, drained, oil reserved
180g unsmoked streaky bacon, roughly chopped
2 garlic cloves, finely chopped
100g sundried or SunBlush tomatoes, chopped
2 tbsp fresh flat-leaf parsley, chopped
1 large red chilli, halved, deseeded and finely chopped
2 tbsp freshly grated Parmesan, to serve (optional)

Prepare 30 minutes
Cook 30 minutes

1 Cook the pasta in a large pan of lightly salted boiling water for 8-10 minutes, or according to the timings on the packet, until al dente.

2 Meanwhile, heat 2 tbsp of the reserved artichoke oil in a frying pan and fry the bacon for 3-4 minutes until crisp. Add the garlic, then remove from the heat.

3 Drain the pasta well, then return to the pan and stir in the cooked bacon and garlic, together with the artichokes, sundried or SunBlush tomatoes, parsley and chilli, and season to taste. Divide among four bowls and serve sprinkled with the Parmesan, if using.

"We use a couple of tablespoons of the oil from the artichokes to intensify the flavour."

Gordon 's tip

Moroccan chicken skewers with parsley, almond & feta salad

If you cook only one dish from this cookbook, this is it. The intriguing blend of the salty-sweet salad, almonds and chicken, with its smoky Moroccan spices, produces a dish chock-full of protein. You'll find that it works fantastically well with monkfish, too. If you like, try including prunes or apricots in the salad.

Serves 6

For the spice rub:
1 tbsp coriander seeds
2 tsp cumin seeds
1 cinnamon stick, crushed
6 whole cloves
¼ tsp saffron strands
1½ tsp ground turmeric
2 large garlic cloves, crushed
Finely grated zest of 1 lemon
3 tbsp olive oil, plus extra to serve
1 tsp salt
12 skinless, boneless chicken thigh
    fillets (about 1kg)
Lemon wedges, to serve

For the parsley salad:
3 tbsp extra virgin olive oil
2 tsp red wine vinegar
Salt and freshly ground black pepper
Large bunch flat-leaf parsley, leaves
    only
200g feta, crumbled
100g blanched Marcona almonds,
    toasted and chopped
100g pitted dates, chopped

Prepare 30 minutes, plus marinating
Cook 14-16 minutes

1 Soak 12 bamboo skewers in a bowl of cold water for 30 minutes.

2 Make the spice rub by dry-frying the coriander seeds, cumin seeds, crushed cinnamon stick, cloves and saffron in a frying pan for 2-3 minutes until they start to release their aroma. Cool slightly, tip into a spice grinder and grind to a powder. Mix in the turmeric, garlic, lemon zest, oil and salt.

3 Cut the chicken thighs in half, place in a bowl and rub in the spice mixture to coat them. Cover and place in the fridge to marinate for at least 20 minutes, but ideally overnight.

4 Thread 2 chicken thigh pieces on to each skewer and cook on a hot griddle pan for 12-13 minutes, turning halfway through, until the chicken is thoroughly cooked with no pink meat and the juices run clear.

5 Meanwhile, make the salad. Whisk together the oil, vinegar and some salt and pepper in a large bowl. Add the parsley, feta, almonds and dates and toss well. Transfer to a platter, squeeze over some of the juice from the lemon wedges and drizzle with a little extra olive oil. Serve 2 chicken skewers per person with a mound of the salad.

Sirloin steak with basil cream sauce

This is a straightforward recipe that couldn't be any faster, which means it's perfect for midweek suppers. It also works very well with more economical cuts such as rump or skirt.

Serves 4

4 British beef sirloin steaks
Salt and freshly ground black pepper
2 tbsp unsalted butter
2 tsp olive oil, plus extra to drizzle
400g tagliatelle
4 shallots, finely chopped
200ml dry white wine
4 tomatoes, skinned, deseeded and chopped (see tip, below)
200ml tub half-fat crème fraîche
Small bunch fresh basil

Prepare 20 minutes
Cook 10-20 minutes

1 Trim the fat off the meat and season both sides of the steaks with freshly ground black pepper. Melt the butter and oil in a medium frying pan over a moderate heat and fry the steaks for 4-5 minutes for rare, 8-10 minutes for medium and 10-12 minutes for well done, turning just once during cooking. Remove from the pan, put on a plate and cover to keep warm.

2 Cook the tagliatelle in a large pan of lightly salted boiling water for 12 minutes, or according to the packet instructions, until al dente. Drain well, season and toss in a little olive oil.

3 Add the shallots to the pan with a drizzle of oil and cook for 2-3 minutes until softened, then pour in the wine, bring to the boil and simmer to reduce by half. Stir in the tomatoes and crème fraîche and simmer for 1-2 minutes, while you shred the basil. Reduce the heat and stir in the basil. Season to taste.

4 Serve the steaks on a bed of tagliatelle, with the sauce poured over the top.

"To skin the tomatoes, cut a small cross on the base, place in a bowl, cover them with boiling water and leave for 1 minute. Drain and cool slightly. The skins will be easy to peel." **James B's tip**

Cod baked with sweet chilli & coriander

Try this sublimely simple way of doing a Thai version of baked cod: it's packed full of zingy, spicy, citrusy flavours, so you'll be serving up a tasty, as well as healthy, dish.

Serves 4

Small bunch fresh coriander, roughly chopped
2 large red chillies, halved, deseeded and finely chopped
4 tbsp olive oil
Finely grated zest and juice of 2 limes
2 tbsp clear honey
2-4 tbsp soy sauce
4 tsp Thai fish sauce
4 x 150g cod fillets, skinned
600g fresh egg noodles

Prepare 30 minutes
Cook 20 minutes

1 Preheat the oven to 220°C/200°C fan oven/gas mark 7. Put half the coriander in a bowl and add the chillies, olive oil, lime zest and juice, honey, soy and fish sauce. Mix everything together.

2 Place the cod in a non-stick roasting tin. Pour the coriander and chilli mixture over the top. Roast in the oven for 8-10 minutes or until the cod is opaque and thoroughly cooked.

3 Meanwhile, cook the noodles in a pan of boiling water according to the packet instructions and drain into a colander.

4 Toss the cooked noodles in the juices in the roasting tin and add the remaining coriander. Adjust the seasoning to taste with extra soy, fish sauce and lime juice if you like. Divide the noodles between four warmed plates and arrange the cod on top.

"This dish works equally well using sea bass and halibut instead of cod."

Wilson's tip

Spanish-style chicken with chorizo & chickpeas

A great one-pot roast that's perfect as a midweek meal when you need something fast.

Serves 6

800g chicken thighs
250g cooking chorizo, cut into
    large chunks
2 red onions, cut into wedges
6 garlic cloves, skins on
¼ tsp flaked sea salt
1 tsp smoked paprika
1 tbsp extra virgin olive oil
400g can chopped tomatoes
400g can chickpeas, drained and
    rinsed
Few sprigs flat-leaf parsley, roughly
    chopped

Prepare 5 minutes
Cook 45 minutes

1 Preheat the oven to 200°C/180°C fan oven/gas mark 6. Put the chicken in a large, non-stick roasting tin with the chorizo, onions, garlic and salt. Sprinkle with the paprika, season, then drizzle with the oil and rub everything together well. Make sure the chicken pieces are all skin side up.

2 Roast for 30 minutes, then stir the tomatoes and chickpeas around the chicken.

3 Return to the oven for 15 minutes, after which time the chicken should be crisp on top and cooked through with no sign of any pink flesh. Scatter over the parsley and serve with crusty bread.

> **Wine suggestion**
> With its rich, nutty character and smoky oak, a terrific white Rioja is a great match with spicy Spanish flavours.

"This is a great standby dish to freeze and have ready for unexpected guests."

Gordon's tip

Baked trout with rosemary & ginger

This is another winner from our Simple Suppers course that everyone raves about. Trout is an excellent source of protein and, because its fat and oils are distributed throughout the flesh, rather than just in the liver (as in white fish), it provides a mega hit of omega-3, the oil that helps reduce cholesterol, protect the heart and boost brain function, too.

Serves 4

Olive oil, for drizzling
800g fresh trout fillets, skinned
Salt and freshly ground black pepper
5 sprigs fresh rosemary, finely
    chopped
Small bunch fresh flat-leaf parsley,
    chopped
2 pieces thumb-size root ginger, very
    finely minced
450g baby spinach
50g pine nuts, toasted

For the dressing:
2 tbsp clear honey
Finely grated zest and juice of ½
    orange
Juice of ¼ lemon
1 tsp soy sauce

Prepare 10 minutes
Cook 25 minutes

1 Preheat the oven to 200°C/180°C fan oven/gas mark 6. Lightly oil an ovenproof dish.

2 Put the trout fillets on a board and slice in half lengthways. Season lightly on both sides. Cut the halves in half through the middle to give 8 smaller pieces. Mix together the rosemary, parsley and minced ginger in a bowl and season.

3 Spread the herb mixture over one half of the trout fillets, then put the other half on top and sandwich together. Drizzle over a little olive oil, season then place in the ovenproof dish. Bake for about 15 minutes or until the fish is opaque and flakes with a fork.

4 Meanwhile, make the dressing by mixing together in a small bowl the honey, orange zest and juice, lemon juice, soy sauce and a little seasoning.

5 In a large saucepan, lightly cook the spinach for 2–3 minutes until it has wilted, then stir through the pine nuts and season lightly.

6 Divide the spinach and pine nuts between four warmed serving plates and top each pile of spinach with a piece of fish. Pour the dressing over and serve with steamed rice.

"Try substituting a piece of salmon for the trout or, when it's in season, curly kale for the spinach, if you like." **Jon's tip**

Classic tomato soup with Welsh rarebit

Is there anything more satisfying than this combination of homemade tomato soup and the indulgent delight of melted cheese with a kick? It was invented over 200 years ago and is loved as much now as it was then.

Serves 4

For the tomato soup:
4 tbsp olive oil
2 medium onions, finely chopped
6 garlic cloves, finely chopped
2 tsp fresh thyme, finely chopped
2 tbsp tomato purée
2 x 400g cans chopped tomatoes
500ml chicken stock
100g roasted red peppers in oil (such as piquillo), drained and roughly chopped
Salt and freshly ground black pepper
Pinch sugar
Small bunch fresh flat-leaf parsley, finely chopped

For the Welsh rarebit:
225g extra mature Cheddar, grated
25g butter, melted
1 tbsp Worcestershire sauce
1 tbsp English mustard
1 tbsp plain flour
4 tbsp bitter or pale ale or dry cider
Cayenne pepper, to taste
White pepper, to taste
2 tbsp tomato chutney (optional)
6 slices bread, brown or white

Prepare 20 minutes
Cook 40 minutes

1 To make the soup, heat the olive oil in a large saucepan over a medium heat. Cook the onions for 3-4 minutes, then add the garlic and thyme and sauté for a further 3-4 minutes or until the onion is transparent. Add the tomato purée and cook, stirring continuously, for 3 minutes.

2 Add the chopped tomatoes and stock and bring to the boil. Reduce the heat, cover and simmer for 15-20 minutes, adding a little extra stock or water if necessary.

3 Stir in the roasted peppers and pour the soup into a blender. Whiz to a smooth purée, pour back into the pan and season to taste. Add the sugar and stir in the parsley. Keep warm while you make the Welsh rarebit.

4 To make the rarebit, preheat the grill to high. Mix together all the ingredients except the chutney and bread. Toast the bread until lightly golden on each side. Spread one side of each slice thinly with the chutney (if using), then spread the cheese mixture thickly on top.

5 Place on a baking sheet and grill for 8 minutes until golden. Serve immediately with the tomato soup.

Entertaining at home 3

Salad of nectarine, mozzarella & tomato with Parma ham

Claire, one of our teachers at the cookery school, made this salad as part of her interview and even brought her own oil from her dad's farm in Italy! No surprise that she won a place on the team. Its fresh ingredients make it a terrific summer dish, with nectarines and tomatoes providing an easy way to get at least one of your five a day.

Serves 4

1-2 seasonal crisp lettuce, such as cos or little gem, roughly torn

4 ripe nectarines, stoned and quartered

250g assorted ripe tomatoes (such as Red Choice, San Marzano, yellow cherry), halved or quartered

2 x 250g balls buffalo mozzarella, torn into quarters

6 slices Parma ham, torn into strips

Salt and freshly ground black pepper

Handful fresh basil, torn

Extra virgin olive oil, for drizzling

Balsamic vinegar, to taste

Few drops lemon juice, to taste

Prepare 15 minutes

1 Scatter the prepared lettuce, nectarines, tomatoes, mozzarella and Parma ham randomly in a single layer on a large platter. Season lightly with salt and a few twists of black pepper.

2 Scatter over the fresh basil and drizzle with the olive oil, balsamic vinegar and lemon juice. This salad should be served just cooler than room temperature, but not as cold as the fridge.

"This salad relies on the quality and freshness of the ingredients, so make it in the summer when tomatoes and nectarines are at their peak of flavour. Use melon instead of nectarine during the winter months."

Claire's tip

"Preheating the baking tray will give you crisp puff pastry on both top and bottom."

James B's tip

Venison en croûte

Using venison instead of beef is a twist on the French classic, *filet de boeuf en croûte*. In English, it's called 'Beef Wellington', which might just have been a patriotic rebranding, after the duke of the same name. He was reputedly uninterested in food, but this was one of the few dishes to tempt him. Venison is a healthy meat option, as wild game is very lean.

Serves 4

4 x 120g venison loin steaks
2 tbsp olive oil
Salt and freshly ground black pepper
40g butter
200g button mushrooms, finely sliced
100g chicken liver pâté
4 slices Serrano ham
2 tbsp plain flour, for dusting
600g ready-rolled puff pastry
2 medium egg yolks, beaten

Prepare 30 minutes
Cook 15–20 minutes

Wine suggestion
There's nothing better with venison than a rich, gamey red, especially when it's combined with mushrooms and pâté. Try wines made from the Mourvèdre grape (such as Bandol, Californian blends or Châteauneuf-du-Pape), or a richer Pinot Noir, ideally with some age.

---

1 Preheat the oven to 220°C/200°C fan oven/gas mark 7, and place a baking tray inside.

2 Preheat a non-stick frying pan. Brush the venison steaks lightly with a little of the oil. When the pan is smoking hot, add the venison and cook on each side for 30 seconds to seal. Remove from the pan, season lightly then place on clean, dry kitchen paper on a plate and put in the fridge to chill.

3 In the same pan, melt the butter with the remaining oil and fry the mushrooms over a high heat until caramelised and just cooked. Season to taste then drain and chill until needed.

4 Place the pâté in a bowl and beat with a spatula to soften. Add the cooked, chilled mushrooms to the pâté and fold through.

5 Spread a slice of Serrano ham with a ½cm thick layer of the pâté-and-mushroom mixture. Place a venison steak on top and wrap the ham around the steak to create a neat parcel. Repeat with the remaining ham, pâté-mushroom mixture and venison steaks to make three more parcels.

6 Lightly dust a piece of parchment paper with plain flour. Unroll the puff pastry and cut four x 15cm rings. Set the rings aside and discard the excess pastry. Brush the rounds with beaten egg yolk, and place a venison parcel on top of each pastry circle. Fold over to create a turnover shape and secure the edges by crimping them with a fork. Trim off the excess pastry, leaving a 1cm border. Brush each venison en croûte liberally with egg yolk and score attractively with a cocktail stick or fork prongs.

7 Place the parcels on the preheated tray and bake for about 12 minutes until lightly crisp and golden. Allow to rest for 5 minutes before serving with steamed cabbage and the Caramelised Onion Gravy (strained to remove the bits) on page 41.

Pan-fried tiger prawns, monkfish & fennel

This is an amazing salad. Monkfish is absolutely perfect for it, and we use large, fat juicy tiger prawns. Alternatively, you can try using scallops and chorizo instead.

Serves 4 (starter or light lunch)

2 x 150g monkfish fillets
2 tbsp extra virgin olive oil
2 tbsp freshly squeezed lemon juice
1 tsp salt
½ tsp black peppercorns, crushed
½ tsp fennel seeds, crushed
½ tsp crushed Kashmiri chilli
Pinch dried chilli flakes
14 raw tiger prawns, peeled
3 tbsp sherry vinegar
100ml clarified butter (see tip opposite)
2 plum tomatoes, deseeded and diced
2 tbsp coarsely chopped dill
125g mixed baby salad leaves

Prepare 30 minutes
Cook 10 minutes

1 Put the monkfish on a board, then trim and discard any membrane from the outside.

2 In a large bowl, mix together the olive oil, lemon juice, salt, peppercorns, fennel seeds, Kashmiri chillies and chilli flakes. Add the monkfish and toss in the mixture.

3 Heat a heavy-based frying pan. Lift the monkfish out of the marinade and cook over a high heat for 2 minutes until lightly brown. Turn the monkfish over and add the tiger prawns. Cook for a further 2 minutes until both are just cooked through.

4 Transfer the monkfish and prawns to a plate and allow the pan to cool slightly. Add the sherry vinegar, remaining marinade and clarified butter, and stir over a low to medium heat to release all the flavours.

5 Add the tomatoes and dill, and season to taste.

6 To serve, slice the monkfish diagonally in 1cm thick slices. Arrange the monkfish, prawns and salad leaves in the centre of four large plates and spoon over the warm dressing. Serve immediately.

"To make clarified butter, gently melt salted butter in a saucepan or heatproof bowl over a very low heat. Leave to stand for a few minutes, then spoon the crusty white layer of salt particles off the top. The clear 'liquid underneath is the clarified butter." **Gordon's tip**

Herb-crusted veal with polenta fries, olive purée & sauce vierge

This is a true example of fine dining from our Michelin Star course. Don't be put off by the long list of ingredients - a lot can be done in advance. The veal and polenta chips give a nod towards Italy, and the fresh sauce vierge, invented by the famous chef Michel Guérard in the 1980s, gives a nod towards France. For tips on how to plate up this classic, see pages 46–47.

Serves 4

4 x 120g veal fillets
2 tbsp olive oil
100g marinated artichoke hearts

For the polenta fries:
140g quick-cook polenta
1½ tbsp butter
2 tbsp finely grated Parmesan
1 tbsp plain flour, for dusting

For the herb crust:
100g fresh breadcrumbs
100g unsalted butter
Small bunch fresh flat-leaf parsley, picked and roughly chopped
20g Parmesan, finely grated, plus 12 large shavings to serve
2 garlic cloves, roughly chopped
Finely grated zest of 1 lemon

For the black olive purée:
200g Kalamata olives, pitted
100ml extra virgin olive oil
1-2 tbsp sherry vinegar

For the sauce vierge:
16 baby plum tomatoes, quartered
Salt and freshly ground black pepper
1 small shallot, very finely diced
1 small garlic clove, minced
Basil, to garnish
1 tbsp sherry vinegar
2-3 tbsp extra virgin olive oil

Prepare 1 hour
Cook 30-40 minutes

1 Preheat the oven to 230°C/210°C fan oven/gas mark 8, and a deep-fat fryer to 190°C.

2 First make the polenta. Bring 600ml cold water with a pinch of salt to the boil in a large saucepan. Tip in the polenta, whisking constantly to prevent lumps forming. Simmer over a medium heat for 5 minutes, still whisking continuously. When the polenta mixture has thickened to the consistency of mashed potato, beat in the butter and Parmesan over a low heat and keep warm. If the polenta dries out, add a little water.

3 Pour into a 450g loaf tin lined with cling film, then cover and chill for 20-30 minutes or until firm (you could do this a day in advance). Turn out the chilled polenta from the tin and cut into chips 5cm x 1cm x 1cm and place in the fridge until needed.

4 To make the herb crust, whiz all the ingredients in a food processor, scraping down the sides of the bowl occasionally, until smooth. Chill.

5 Make the black olive purée by placing all the ingredients in a food processor and blending to a coarse purée. Chill.

6 To make the sauce vierge, place the tomatoes in a bowl. Season lightly, and stir in the shallot, garlic, basil, vinegar and oil. Check the seasoning, then cover and set aside.

7 Preheat a non-stick frying pan until smoking hot. Lightly rub the veal fillets with a little olive oil and sear briefly in the hot pan until caramelised on both sides. Season lightly, then remove from the pan and place on a baking tray. Top each fillet with 1 tbsp of herb crust mixture and spread evenly over the surface.

8 To complete the dish, put the marinated artichoke hearts on the tray with the veal and roast for 5-6 minutes. Remove from the oven and allow to rest, still on the tray.

9 While the veal is cooking, lightly flour the polenta chips and deep-fry until golden brown and crisp. Drain on clean, dry kitchen paper.

10 Arrange the olive purée and polenta fries on four large warm plates — each has 1 tbsp of purée and 3 fries. Place a veal fillet on each plate and top with an artichoke heart. Spoon over the sauce vierge, garnish with Parmesan shavings and basil leaves, and serve.

Butternut soup with Parmesan, pine nuts & sage

This basic soup is wonderfully versatile, as it works very well with other vegetables such as celeriac and Jerusalem artichoke, or any other specialist varieties of pumpkin and squash you may come across.

Serves 4

50g unsalted butter
1 small onion, finely sliced
2 garlic cloves
1 tsp salt
½ medium butternut squash (approx. 400g), peeled, deseeded and finely sliced
500ml chicken stock
Bouquet garni (1 bay leaf, 2 thyme sprigs, 1 small rosemary sprig, 5 black peppercorns)
3 tbsp double cream
12 sage leaves
10g Parmesan, shaved
10g pine nuts, toasted

Prepare 20 minutes
Cook 1 hour 30 minutes

1 Melt half the butter in a large saucepan and sweat the onion and garlic with the salt for about 4-5 minutes until softened. Add the butternut squash and cook for about 10 minutes until very soft. Add the chicken stock and bouquet garni, bring to the boil, then cook for 30 minutes over a low heat. Remove the bouquet garni.

2 Add the double cream, bring back to the boil and blend in a liquidiser until smooth. For a finer texture, pass the soup through a sieve.

3 When ready to serve, reheat the soup and gently fry the sage leaves in the remaining butter until lightly crisped. Serve the soup in warmed bowls and garnish with the Parmesan, toasted pine nuts and crisp sage leaves.

"Serve with warm Gougeres (see the recipe on page 92)."

Gordon's tip

Prawns, fino sherry & garlic

The Spanish know a thing or two about sherry - it has been a major ingredient in their national cuisine for centuries and is regarded with all the reverence accorded to a cultural icon. Here, the sharp dryness of the sherry offsets the olive oil of the fried prawns perfectly.

Serves 3-4

4 tbsp olive oil
450g raw shelled tiger prawns, de-veined
Salt and freshly ground black pepper
3 garlic cloves, finely chopped
Pinch paprika
50ml fino sherry
2 tbsp extra virgin olive oil
Chopped fresh parsley, to serve

Prepare 10 minutes
Cook 12 minutes

1 Heat the olive oil in a frying pan and add the raw shelled tiger prawns. Season with a little salt and cook for 3 minutes, or until they begin to turn pink. Remove from the pan and keep warm.

2 In the same pan, stir in the garlic and the pinch of paprika. Add the sherry and bring to the boil for 1 minute. Add the extra virgin olive oil to the pan, whisking to lightly emulsify the sauce, and return the prawns to warm through.

3 Add the chopped parsley and serve. Mop up the garlicky juices with chunks of crusty artisan loaf.

"A little cooking chorizo makes a fantastic addition to this recipe: pan-fry thin slices while cooking the prawns."

Gordon's tip

Sesame king prawn toasts

These toasts are outstanding – not just because of the exotic mix of flavours, but because they combine two highly nutritious food sources. Sesame seeds add a delicate, nutty, almost imperceptible crunch and are chock-a-block with essential fatty acids, while prawns are packed with protein, yet are low in saturated fat.

Serves 4

600g raw king prawns, peeled, de-veined and roughly chopped
6 spring onions, trimmed and finely sliced
3 tbsp fresh coriander, finely chopped
1 thumb-size chunk fresh root ginger, peeled and minced
1 tsp Shaoxing rice wine or dry sherry
1 tbsp light soy sauce
1 medium egg white
½ tsp salt, plus extra for sprinkling
6 slices thick white bread
100g sesame seeds
1-2 litres vegetable oil, for deep-frying

Prepare 15-20 minutes
Cook 5 minutes

1 Place the prawns in a blender with the spring onions, coriander, ginger, rice wine or sherry, soy sauce, egg white and salt. Whiz to blend everything into a coarse mixture.

2 On a board, remove and discard the crusts from the bread and cut each slice in half diagonally. Put about 1 tbsp of the prawn mixture on to each piece of bread, lightly pressing the mixture to cover well. Gently roll each piece of prawn bread in sesame seeds to lightly coat.

3 Heat the vegetable oil in a deep-fat fryer to 190°C. Working in batches, carefully lower the prawn bread, prawn side down, into the hot oil and fry for approximately 1 minute. Turn the toasts over and cook on the other side for a further 1 minute, or until lightly browned all over and just cooked through. Remove the toasts from the fryer using a slotted spoon and transfer to a plate lined with kitchen paper to drain. Sprinkle with salt.

4 Serve immediately with a bowl of sweet chilli dipping sauce (see page 44).

"Make sure your oil is at the right temperature before deep-frying — if it's too cold, the toasts will absorb too much oil."

Wilson's tip

Pork & pistachio terrine

Terrines are chunky, highly flavoured pâté mixtures baked in rectangular crocks. The sky's the limit as far as ingredients go, as their big selling point is their potential for imaginative versatility (see the tip below). Here, pork and pistachio go together as though they were meant for one another.

Serves 6-8

20g butter
2 large banana shallots, finely diced
1 garlic clove, finely chopped
4 sprigs thyme, picked
225g pork belly, minced
225g lean veal, minced
220g chicken livers, half minced, half roughly chopped
2 tsp brandy
50g pistachio nuts, shelled and toasted
Pinch allspice
Salt and freshly ground black pepper
225g streaky bacon
2 bay leaves

Prepare 20 minutes
Cook 1 hour 45 minutes

1 Preheat the oven to 150°C/130°C fan oven/gas mark 2. Melt the butter in a pan and cook the shallots, garlic and thyme until very soft. Allow to cool.

2 Mix the pork, veal and chicken livers with the cooked shallot mixture, and then mix in the brandy, pistachios and allspice, and season with salt and pepper.

3 Line a 500g terrine mould with the bacon rashers. Tip in the prepared mixture, press flat and fold over the rashers. Lay the bay leaves on top.

4 Cover the terrine with foil and place in a roasting tin in the oven and pour enough boiling water into the tin to come halfway up the sides. Cook in the oven for 1½ hours.

5 When it's cooked, remove from the oven, allow to cool and then refrigerate for at least 1 day.

6 To serve, cut the terrine into generous slices and accompany with toast, butter, pickles and chutney.

Wine suggestion
The best wine for this dish depends on the occasion and how much of the chutney you use. You could try a robust red such as a Touriga blend from Portugal, or a Côtes du Rhône-Villages. If you're serving it as a lighter meal with lots of the chutney and a green salad, a German Riesling would work well.

"Prunes make a nice addition to the terrine: just add 100g roughly chopped pitted prunes to the mixture at Step 2 for a little extra sweetness." **James B's tip**

Entertaining at home

Endive salad with pear, Roquefort & sweet mustard dressing

This is a real French classic inspired by a recipe from Bofinger, one of the oldest brasseries in Paris. It's a magical combination of sweet, salty, bitter flavours with deliciously creamy, crunchy textures. We've added the red wine-poached pears to celebrate one of our favourite autumnal fruits.

Serves 4

For the poached pear:
200ml red wine
100ml port
4 tsp red wine vinegar
60g sugar
2 ripe pears, peeled, cored and cut
    into 12-16 wedges

For the salad:
8 heads endive
100g Roquefort, crumbled
100g toasted walnuts, coarsely
    chopped
Small bunch fresh flat-leaf parsley,
    finely chopped

For the sweet mustard dressing:
50g wholegrain mustard
2 tbsp Dijon mustard
50g sugar
2 tbsp white wine vinegar
4 tbsp vegetable oil

Prepare 10 minutes
Cook 5-10 minutes

1 Heat the red wine, port, vinegar and sugar together in a large pan until the sugar has dissolved. Add the pear wedges and simmer for 5-10 minutes, turning halfway through, until tender. Leave to cool.

2 Trim the root from the endive and separate the leaves. Combine them with the Roquefort, walnuts and parsley in a salad bowl.

3 To make the dressing, whisk both mustards, the sugar and vinegar with 2 tsp water. Once these are combined, slowly incorporate the oil, whisking continuously. Dress the salad with 2-3 tbsp of the dressing.

4 Divide the salad between four bowls and garnish with slices of the poached pear.

"For a lighter touch, serve the salad with segments of juicy orange. To enjoy the sweet mustard dressing with smoked salmon or mackerel, add a little finely chopped dill to it."

James B's tip

Chicken breast with pancetta, broad beans & herb mascarpone

This recipe is reminiscent of the fantastic fusion cooking you find in Australia. It's the clever balance of sweet and savoury ingredients that makes the dish such a delight. What's more, broad beans are a nutrition powerhouse among the legume family, brilliant for digestive health, as they provide fibre along with useful amounts of minerals.

Serves 4

25ml good-quality balsamic vinegar
1 star anise
50ml olive oil, plus extra for frying
Finely grated zest and juice of 1
    lemon
2 garlic cloves, crushed
2 tsp chopped fresh lemon thyme
½ tsp crushed fennel seeds
4 corn-fed chicken breast fillets, skin on
4 thin slices pancetta
200g broad beans, podded
100g mixed leaves (such as rocket,
    ruby chard and spinach)
Salt and freshly ground black pepper
2 baby gem lettuces, leaves picked
    and cut lengthways

For the herb mascarpone:

3 tbsp fresh flat-leaf parsley,
    finely chopped
1 tbsp fresh chives, finely
    chopped
3 tbsp fresh basil leaves, finely
    chopped
1 tbsp fresh oregano, finely
    chopped
Finely grated zest and juice of 1
    lemon
250g mascarpone
2 tbsp extra virgin olive oil

Prepare 40 minutes, plus marinating
Cook 25-30 minutes

1 Place the balsamic vinegar in a pan with the star anise and warm slightly on a low heat. Remove from the heat and set aside to infuse while you carry on.

2 Make a marinade by combining the olive oil, lemon zest and juice, garlic, thyme and fennel seeds in a large, shallow sealable container and add the chicken, skin side up. Don't cover the skin with the marinade - leaving it exposed and dry will help it go crispy. Cover and place in the fridge for a minimum of 6 hours to marinate.

3 Prepare the herb mascarpone by mixing all the ingredients together in a bowl with 2 tbsp cold water, gently folding it through the mixture. Place in the fridge until needed.

4 Preheat the oven to 200°C/180°C fan oven/gas mark 6. Heat a heavy-based ovenproof pan on a high heat and add a little oil. Wipe the marinade off the chicken with some clean, dry kitchen paper and place the chicken in the pan skin side down. Fry for 3-5 minutes, turning once or twice or until well coloured on both sides. Place the pan in the oven for a further 8-10 minutes or until the chicken is thoroughly cooked, there is no pink meat and the skin is crisp and golden. When cooked, remove the chicken from the oven, pour off any excess fat, then leave to rest for 5-6 minutes.

5 Meanwhile, spread the pancetta out on to a baking tray and bake in the oven alongside the chicken for 4-5 minutes until crisp. Remove and keep warm.

6 Remove the chicken from the pan and place on a chopping board. Put the pan back on a low heat, add the broad beans and warm through. Add the mixed leaves and stir through. Season with a little salt and pepper and add to a bowl along with the baby gem lettuce and toss well. Divide the mixture evenly between four plates.

7 Slice the chicken in half and place on top of the bean and leaf mixture. Spoon a little of the warm balsamic vinegar over the chicken, top with a tablespoon of the herb mascarpone and garnish with the crisp pancetta.

"Any leftover herb mascarpone will keep in the fridge for up to 3 days. It's delicious served with the Southern-fried chicken (see page 199)."

Gordon's tip

Gougères

These delicious savoury cheese puffs are great with any wine or champagne - they also make terrific canapés or hors d'oeuvres for a party. Make plenty, as they're addictive.

Makes 25-30 canapés

60ml whole milk
½ tsp salt
50g unsalted butter, diced
75g plain flour, well sifted
2 medium eggs
100g Comté cheese, finely grated

Prepare 20 minutes
Cook 20 minutes

1 Preheat the oven to 220°C/200°C fan oven/gas mark 7. Pour the milk into a heavy-based saucepan. Add the salt, butter and 60ml water. Place over a medium heat and allow the butter to melt. Add the flour. Lower the heat and stir the mixture together quickly to make a smooth paste. The mixture is ready when it looks shiny and cleanly leaves the sides of the pan. Take off the heat and allow to cool until lukewarm.

2 With the pan off the heat, beat each egg into the mixture until it looks glossy and shiny. Stir in 75g of the grated cheese. Pipe or spoon ping-pong ball-sized amounts of the mixture on to baking sheets, leaving a generous gap between each to allow them to spread. Top each mound with a little of the remaining cheese. Bake for about 15 minutes until they have puffed up and look golden and crisp. Transfer to a wire rack and allow to cool.

"To take the stress out of last-minute preparations, make the gougeres on the morning of your dinner party and reheat them gently in the evening when you're ready to serve. This mixture would also make 15 larger gougeres to accompany a meal."

James B's tip

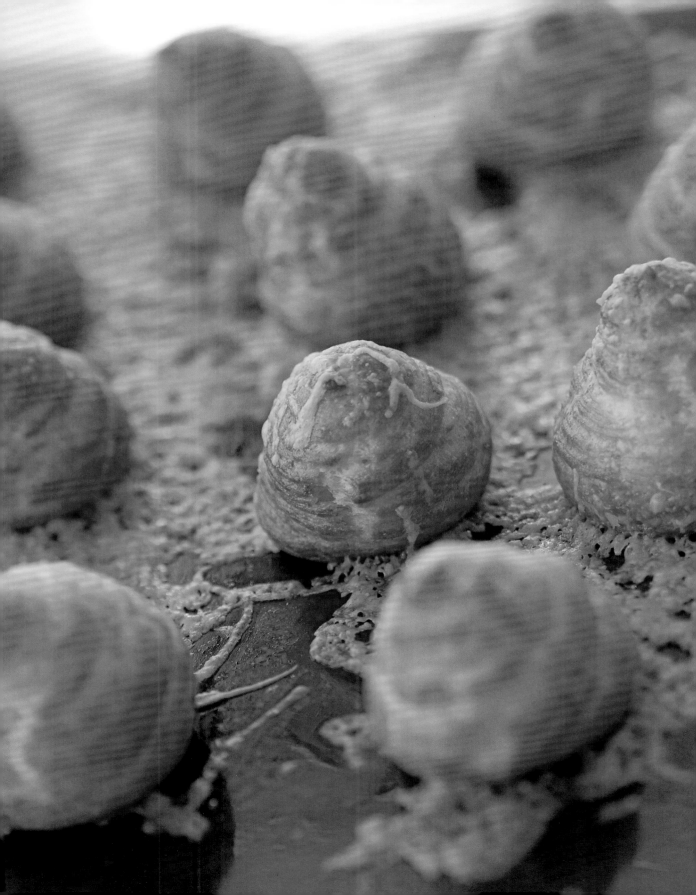

Smoked salmon with pickled ginger, fresh herbs & lemon soy dressing

This is a modern, fusion-style approach to food that's almost Japanese in feel. It began life as a starter, but everyone seems to love it as a dainty canapé. You can feel virtuous enjoying it, too, as Asian-style dressings tend to be lower in fat than their European counterparts, while salmon contains brain-boosting omega-3.

Serves 6

100g sliced smoked salmon
(You will also need 12 Chinese
    porcelain spoons)

For the lemon soy dressing:
2 tbsp caster sugar
Juice and zest of 2 lemons
½ stick lemongrass, crushed
2 tbsp olive oil
1 tsp light soy sauce

To serve:
15g pink pickled ginger, drained and
    roughly chopped
1 spring onion, trimmed and finely
    sliced at an angle
½ large red chilli, deseeded and finely
    chopped
1 tsp fresh mint, leaves picked and
    washed
1 tsp fresh coriander, leaves picked
    and washed
1 tsp fresh dill, picked and washed

Prepare 15 minutes, plus chilling
Cook 5 minutes

1 Remove the salmon from the fridge 20 minutes before serving. Tear the fish into bite-size pieces and spread evenly over a large plate. You can do this a day in advance, cover with cling film and put back in the fridge.

2 To make the dressing, put the sugar, lemon juice, lemon zest, lemongrass and 4 tbsp water into a pan and bring to the boil. Simmer for 5 minutes or until it begins to thicken to a syrupy consistency. Remove from the heat, allow to cool slightly then place in the fridge. When completely cool, add the olive oil and soy sauce and whisk together thoroughly. Remove the lemongrass and set aside until ready to use.

3 Put a little portion of the salmon into each canapé spoon. Drizzle a little dressing over the salmon, scatter over the ginger, some spring onion, a couple of pieces of chilli and one leaf each of mint, coriander and dill, and serve immediately.

Blueberry caipirinha, Espresso martini and Japanese slipper cocktails

This is Brazil's national cocktail, made with cachaça, a local sugar cane rum. ('Caipirinha' comes from *caipira*, which means 'hillbilly' in Portuguese!)

Caipirinha

6-7 blueberries, plus a few extra to garnish
2-3 tsp brown sugar, or to taste
½ lime, cut into 4 wedges
5-6 mint leaves, plus a few extra sprigs to garnish
50ml cachaça
25ml soda water, approx

Serves 1
Ready 1-2 minutes

1 Place the blueberries, sugar, lime and mint in a cocktail shaker. Mix well for 20-30 seconds until the blueberries are crushed and the lime is soft.

2 Add ice and cachaça, replace the top of the cocktail shaker and shake hard for 10-15 seconds.

3 Pour the contents of the cocktail shaker into a rocks glass (a short tumbler), top with soda water and garnish with a sprig of mint and the extra blueberries speared on a cocktail stick.

The real depth of flavour of this cocktail offsets the sweetness perfectly.

Espresso martini

Ice
30ml freshly brewed espresso coffee
30ml vodka
30ml Kahlua (or other coffee liqueur)
Few coffee beans, to serve

Serves 1
Ready 2 minutes

1 Heap plenty of ice into a martini glass. This will help keep the cocktail chilled without diluting it.

2 Fill a cocktail shaker three-quarters full with ice. Pour the coffee, vodka and Kahlua or other coffee liqueur into the shaker, put the top on and shake for 8-10 seconds.

3 Tip the ice out of the martini glass. Strain the cocktail into the glass and float a few coffee beans on top to garnish. Serve straightaway.

One of our teachers, Wilson, concocted this. It's a violent green that stops you in your tracks until you taste it and realise that it's simply sublime.

Japanese slipper

Ice
30ml Midori melon liqueur
30ml Cointreau (or Triple Sec)
30ml freshly squeezed lemon juice
Glacé cherry, burnt lemon peel or lemon zest, to serve

Serves 1
Ready 2 minutes

1 Put some ice into a martini glass to chill it while you make the cocktail (this will help keep the drink cold without diluting it with more ice).

2 Fill a cocktail shaker with ice. Pour in the Midori, Cointreau and lemon juice. Secure the lid on the cocktail shaker and shake for 8-10 seconds.

3 Tip the ice out of the martini glass and strain the cocktail into it. Garnish with a glacé cherry, burnt lemon peel (see tip opposite) or lemon zest.

"To make burnt lemon peel, just shave a small piece of peel from a lemon, put it on a plate, and run the flame of a lit match or lighter over it for 10 seconds."

Wilson's tip

Asian 4

Green papaya & tamarind salad

This should taste hot, spicy, sour and sweet all at the same time. Papaya is an excellent source of vitamins A and C, which makes it the star of this dish. The Thais eat it with just about everything you can think of – chicken, prawns, pork and more, but they tend to add a lot of chilli, so don't hold back, it needs a kick.

Serves 4 as a side salad

1 small green (under-ripe) papaya
1 tbsp palm sugar or light
  muscovado sugar
1 small garlic clove, chopped
1 red chilli, halved, deseeded and
  finely chopped
5 French beans, halved lengthways
Small handful unsalted peanuts
1 tbsp dried shrimps (optional)
½ tbsp Thai fish sauce
1 tbsp tamarind paste
1 plum tomato, roughly chopped
Juice of 2 limes

Prepare 20 minutes

1 Peel the papaya, then, using a mandolin, turn it into long thin ribbons (you can use a potato peeler for this and then just cut it into strips) – you should have about 200g. Work your way around the fruit until you get to the core and seeds, which you discard.

2 Moisten the palm sugar (or light muscovado sugar) with a little cold water.

3 Put the garlic, red chilli and French beans into a mortar or mixing bowl and lightly bruise with the pestle or the end of a rolling pin. Add the sugar with the peanuts, dried shrimps, fish sauce, tamarind paste, tomato and lime juice, and bruise everything once more, turning the mixture over with a fork as you do so.

4 Add the papaya strips and toss the mixture together, then continue to pound it. The salad is ready when the papaya has been bruised enough to make it look translucent. Serve immediately.

"If green papaya is hard to get hold of, carrot is a good substitute."

Jon's tip

Aromatic Thai duck curry

This is a deliciously fragrant dish - take your time blending the ingredients to get a really smooth paste. There's an unmistakably Indian influence from the Kashmiri chillies, which give the dish a wonderfully dark, aromatic and smoky flavour that partners perfectly with the duck. Removing the skin from the duck reduces the fat content, and you can switch to half-fat coconut milk if you want to be good.

Serves 4

For the curry:

4 Kashmiri chillies

½ tsp salt

1 banana shallot, roughly chopped

6 garlic cloves

4cm piece fresh root ginger, peeled

1 lemongrass stalk

15 white peppercorns

1 tbsp coriander seeds, roasted and ground

2 tsp cumin seeds, roasted and ground

1 tsp fennel seeds, roasted and ground

3 pieces mace, roasted and ground

3 tbsp coconut cream

1 tbsp vegetable oil

1 tbsp palm sugar or light muscovado

3 tbsp Thai fish sauce

400ml can coconut milk

2 duck breasts, skin removed, cut into 3cm cubes

3 medium-sized potatoes, cut into 3cm cubes and cooked until tender

For the garnish:

Vegetable oil, for deep-frying

2 banana shallots, finely sliced

Pinch caster sugar

Pinch salt

2 limes, cut into wedges, to serve

Prepare 30 minutes
Cook 20 minutes

1 Preheat the vegetable oil in a deep-fat fryer to 150°C. First make the garnish. Deep-fry the shallots until crisp and golden, then drain on clean, dry kitchen paper and season with the sugar and a little salt.

2 To make the curry paste, blend together all the ingredients down to and including the mace in a food processor or blender until smooth – this will take about 4-5 minutes. If necessary, add a little water to help the blending process. Add the coconut cream and blend again to combine fully.

3 Heat the vegetable oil in a large saucepan, add the curry paste and fry for at least 5-6 minutes until fragrant.

4 Stir in the palm sugar and fish sauce and add the coconut milk. Bring to a simmer and add the duck and potatoes. Turn down the heat and simmer on a low heat for about 7 minutes, until the duck is tender.

5 Serve the curry in large bowls, sprinkled with the crisp shallots and a lime wedge on the side.

"Thai Coconut Rice and Cucumber Relish (see pages 108–109) go wonderfully with this curry – serve separately in small bowls."

Gordon's tip

Chilli caramel chicken with hot & sour salad

At first glance, this recipe looks daunting, but don't be put off, because you can do so much of it in advance and then heat it up when you need it. What really gives this dish its X factor is the whisky in the sauce - it imparts real depth and a roundness of flavour.

Serves 4

For the chilli caramel chicken:
20ml sunflower oil
1 tsp sea salt
½ tsp freshly ground black pepper
½ tsp ground chilli
2 chicken breasts with skin
12 small dried chillies
2 tbsp tamarind paste
200g palm sugar
150ml scotch whisky
4 garlic cloves, minced
4 small red chillies, minced
Finely grated zest of 2 limes
75ml Thai fish sauce
Juice of 1 lime
120g beansprouts, trimmed

For the hot and sour salad dressing:
Juice of 2 limes
½ tsp chilli oil
Few drops sesame oil
1 tsp Thai fish sauce
1 tbsp tamarind paste
1 tbsp palm sugar or light
    muscovado sugar

For the hot and sour salad:
Small bunch coriander, leaves picked
Small bunch mint, leaves picked
Small bunch basil, leaves picked
6 French beans, sliced small
1 small fennel bulb, shaved into fine rounds
4 spring onions, roughly chopped
1cm fresh root ginger, cut into thin
    matchsticks
2 green bird's-eye chillies, sliced into
    fine rounds
1 long green chilli, deseeded and
    sliced into fine lengths
2 large shallots, finely sliced
4 Chinese cabbage leaves, finely
    shredded
100g beansprouts, trimmed

For the garnish:
1 large shallot, finely sliced
Small bunch basil
Vegetable oil, for deep-frying

Prepare I hour
Cook 30 minutes

1 Preheat the oven to 200°C/180°C fan oven/gas mark 6. Put the sunflower oil, salt, pepper, ground chilli and chicken in a small bowl and toss to coat. Place the chicken in a roasting tin, skin side up, and roast for 10 minutes. Turn over and roast for another 8 minutes or until the chicken is tender and golden.

2 Meanwhile, make the garnish. Preheat a deep-fryer to 190°C. Deep-fry the shallot for 30 seconds, then add the basil for 20 seconds and fry until crisp. Drain on clean, dry kitchen towel and season with a little salt. Set aside. Deep-fry the dried chillies (for the caramel chicken) for 40 seconds and set aside separately.

3 To make the chilli caramel, put the tamarind paste, palm sugar and half the whisky in a saucepan, and bring to the boil. Turn down the heat and add the garlic, minced chilli and lime zest and simmer for 10 minutes or until the mixture begins to thicken and turn brown.

4 Add the fish sauce and dried chillies and simmer for a further 5 minutes until reduced by a third.

5 Add the remaining whisky and bring back to the boil. Reduce the

"Try substituting pork for chicken – I'd recommend using fillet or a thick-cut loin, which works really well."

Jon's tip

mixture to a simmer, stir in the lime juice and remove from the heat. The sauce should now have the colour and consistency of runny honey.

6 Cut the chicken into small chunks, add to the sauce and simmer for 2 minutes. Then add the beansprouts, stir through and remove from the heat.

7 To make the salad dressing, put the lime juice in a large bowl. Add the chilli oil, sesame oil, fish sauce, tamarind paste, sugar and 2 tbsp water and mix well to combine. Then add all the salad ingredients, toss well and divide between four plates.

8 Arrange the caramelised chicken on top, scatter with the fried shallot slices and basil leaves and serve immediately.

King prawn pad Thai

This recipe is for two people, as it's unwieldy to cook for a larger group - you'd need a huge wok and the logistics would be challenging. Crushed, roasted peanuts are the essence of Pad Thai. Roasting liberates the oils, which adds flavour and texture. Make sure the wok is incredibly hot and that you have all the ingredients ready in advance, as you need to cook it quickly.

Serves 2

75g dried medium rice noodles
50g firm tofu, diced into 1cm pieces
1 tbsp palm sugar or light
    muscovado sugar
1 tbsp caster sugar
1 tbsp tamarind paste
2 tbsp Thai fish sauce
1 tbsp groundnut oil
1 large banana shallot, finely sliced
2 garlic cloves, finely sliced
6 large raw tiger prawns, peeled,
    de-veined and halved lengthways
1 medium egg
1 tbsp dried shrimp, rinsed and dried
    (optional)
1 tsp chilli powder
1 handful fresh beansprouts
8 spring onions, finely sliced
2 limes
Small bunch fresh coriander, roughly
    chopped
1 tbsp unsalted and roasted
    peanuts, crushed

Prepare 45 minutes, plus soaking
Cook 10 minutes

1 Put the noodles in a bowl and cover with boiling water. Leave to soak for about 25-30 minutes, stirring regularly until soft. Drain well.

2 To make the crispy tofu, heat a deep-fat fryer to 190°C and add the diced tofu. Fry for 1 minute or until a light golden brown. Remove with a slotted spoon and place on kitchen towel to get rid of excess oil. Set aside.

3 Put the palm sugar (or light muscovado sugar) in a small saucepan. Add the caster sugar, tamarind paste and fish sauce and heat gently until the sugar has dissolved.

4 Heat a dry wok until hot, then add the oil - when the oil sloshes easily around in the wok, you'll know it's ready for cooking. Add the shallot and fry until fragrant and beginning to colour. Add the garlic and prawns. Continue to fry for a further 3-4 minutes, allowing the shallot, garlic and prawns to take on a little colour.

5 Crack in the egg and stir to combine. Mix in the tofu, dried shrimp (if using) and drained noodles. Fry over a high heat, allowing the noodles to colour a little.

6 Add the prepared sauce and a pinch of the chilli powder. Simmer for a further 30 seconds to 1 minute.

7 Finally, add the beansprouts and most of the spring onions (reserve some for garnishing). Cook for a further 30 seconds to 1 minute until just wilted. Add the juice of 1 lime and the coriander. Check the seasoning — the noodles should be sweet, sour and salty.

8 To serve, pile the noodles on to plates, sprinkle with the remaining chilli powder and reserved spring onions, then scatter over the crushed roasted peanuts and a few coriander leaves. Cut the remaining lime into wedges and serve alongside.

> **Wine suggestion**
> German Riesling, cooler climate Viognier or even Prosecco will match the sweetness of this dish, as well as refresh and balance the spicy heat.

Thai coconut rice

Hom Mali rice is the same as Thai jasmine rice, and it's recognisable by its unique fragrance. Whether served as rice or turned into rice flour to make noodles, it's an accompaniment to every Thai meal and a good source of starch for anyone with a gluten allergy.

Serves 4

150ml coconut milk
Zest of 1 lime
½ tsp salt
½ tsp sugar
150g Hom Mali rice

Prepare 5 minutes
Cook 30 minutes

1 In a large saucepan combine the coconut milk, 225ml water, lime zest, salt and sugar. Bring to the boil and add the rice. Stir once to combine the ingredients.

2 Bring back to a simmer, stir once more, then turn down the heat to its lowest setting. Simmer the rice for 20 minutes then remove from the heat and allow to stand for a further 10 minutes.

3 Run a fork through the rice to separate the grains, and serve very hot.

Cucumber relish

This is the perfect partner for Thai Coconut Rice and, also, for the Aromatic Thai Duck Curry on page 102. It serves 4, and takes around 10 minutes to prepare and 5 minutes to cook.

Combine 4 tbsp white wine vinegar, 3 tbsp white sugar, 3 tbsp water and a pinch of salt in a pan, and heat gently until the sugar dissolves. Remove from the heat and allow to cool. The dressing should taste sweet and sour. Quarter 1 cucumber lengthways and thinly slice. Put in a bowl with 1 large shallot, halved and finely sliced; a 4cm piece of fresh root ginger, peeled and cut into very thin strips; 1 red chilli, cut into very thin strips; and a bunch of coriander, finely chopped. Pour over the syrup and stir everything together.

Hot & sour fish soup

This soup is a classic example of oriental subtlety, with its balance of flavours unique to Southeast Asian cooking. It's also very healthy and nourishing, and has only 115 calories per serving!

Serves 4

1 large red chilli, halved, deseeded
    and roughly chopped
1 thumb-sized piece ginger, peeled
    and roughly chopped
3 garlic cloves, roughly chopped
6 large shallots, roughly chopped
1 tsp sugar, either palm or light
    muscovado
1½ tbsp tamarind paste
100g fresh squid, cleaned
1 litre chicken stock
2 tbsp Thai fish sauce
75g French beans, topped, tailed and
    cut into small pieces
100g monkfish fillet, cut into thin slices
120g large prawns, peeled and
    de-veined
50g baby leaf spinach
2 tbsp fresh coriander leaves
½ large red chilli, deseeded and cut
    into long, thin strips
2 limes, halved

Prepare 35 minutes
Cook 15 minutes

1 Put the chilli, ginger, garlic, shallots and sugar into a mortar bowl or a food processor and blend to a coarse paste, adding a little of the tamarind paste if necessary.

2 Cut open the body pouch of the squid along the length of one side and score the inner side with the tip of a small, sharp knife into a fine diamond pattern. Cut the squid into approximately 3cm squares.

3 Bring the chicken stock and the rest of the tamarind paste to the boil in a pan. Add the chilli paste mixture and simmer for 10 minutes. Strain through a very fine sieve, then pour back into the pot and bring to the boil again.

4 Add the Thai fish sauce and the beans and simmer for 1 minute, then add the monkfish, squid and prawns and simmer for 1 minute more. Tip in the spinach and simmer for a further minute.

5 Ladle the soup into four warm bowls, scatter over the coriander leaves and red chilli, and serve with half a lime on the side for squeezing over.

"To make it a more substantial dish, prepare 250g of rice noodles according to packet directions, and divide between four warm bowls, then ladle the soup on top."

Gordon's tip

Goan fish curry with coconut & tamarind

Spicy Goan cooking gives a nod to several cultural influences, chief among them the Hindu, Muslim and Portuguese traditions, all of which have had an impact on Goa's cuisine. But one dish they all share - the region's staple - is fish curry and rice, and it's absolutely delicious. Try this with shelled king prawns, too, which makes a particularly opulent version of the dish.

Serves 4

4 x 175g fish fillets, such as pollock, tilapia or sea bass, skin on
Salt

For the Goan masala paste:
½ tsp coriander seeds
½ tsp cumin seeds
1 tbsp black peppercorns
1 tsp fennel seeds
½ tsp cloves
¼ tsp turmeric powder
3 large red chillies, halved, deseeded and roughly chopped
3 garlic cloves, chopped
1 tbsp palm sugar (or light muscovado sugar)
1 tbsp tamarind paste
1 lemongrass stalk
4cm piece fresh root ginger, peeled and roughly chopped
1 tbsp red wine vinegar

For the curry sauce:
2 tbsp groundnut or sunflower oil
½ tsp black mustard seeds
1 tsp cumin seeds
1 tbsp fennel seeds
¼ tsp fenugreek seeds
2 small onions, thinly sliced
½ tsp ground turmeric
4 medium hot red chillies, halved, deseeded and sliced into juliennes
6 curry leaves
400ml coconut milk
2 tsp tamarind paste

To serve:
Fresh coriander sprigs, to garnish

Prepare 30 minutes
Cook 15-20 minutes

1 Lightly salt the fish fillets on both sides with 1 tsp fine salt and set to one side.

2 Make the Goan masala paste. Put the coriander and cumin seeds, peppercorns and fennel seeds with ½ tsp fine salt in a coffee or spice grinder and grind to a fine powder. Place this powder and the remaining masala paste ingredients in a blender or food processor and blend to make a smooth paste.

3 To prepare the sauce, heat the oil in a pan large enough to hold the fish fillets in one layer. Add the black mustard seeds, cumin, fennel and fenugreek seeds and fry for about 30 seconds or until they begin to pop and jump. Turn down the heat, then add the onions and fry until golden.

4 Add the masala paste and turmeric and fry for 3-4 minutes until it becomes aromatic. Add the chillies, curry leaves, coconut milk, tamarind paste, 150ml cold water and a pinch of salt to taste, and simmer for 5 minutes.

5 Gently lower the fish fillets into the sauce and simmer for another 5 minutes or until just cooked. Serve with steamed basmati rice and garnish with coriander.

"The Goan masala paste can be made in advance and kept in an airtight container in the fridge for up to 2 weeks, or in the freezer for up to 3 months."

Gordon's tip

Sweet 'n' sour pork

This is one of the first recipes Wilson brought to the cookery school. His family is Chinese, so these are the fresh, authentic flavours he grew up with and it's so much tastier than the typical takeaway version you get here in Britain. Deep-fry using the right oils - groundnut oil, rapeseed oil, sunflower oil or olive blends all work really well.

Serves 4

For the sweet 'n' sour sauce:

3 spring onions, sliced diagonally into 3cm lengths
6 cherry tomatoes
1 tbsp olive oil
1 tbsp honey
2 tbsp caster sugar
1 tbsp rice wine vinegar
Ground white pepper

For the pork:

3 medium eggs, separated
1 tbsp Chinese five spice powder
Salt
1 tbsp clear honey
1 tbsp Shaoxing rice wine or dry sherry
3-4 dashes Worcestershire sauce
400g pork fillet, diced into 2cm cubes
Vegetable oil, for frying
100g cornflour

Prepare 45 minutes, plus marinating
Cook 40 minutes

1 Preheat a large griddle pan over high heat until very hot. Drizzle the onions and tomatoes with the oil, then place in the hot pan and cook for 3-4 minutes, turning occasionally, until they start to char and are just softened.

2 Transfer the softened onions and tomatoes to a small saucepan set over medium heat. Add the honey, caster sugar, rice wine vinegar and a pinch of white pepper, stir to combine and cook for 2-3 minutes until syrupy. Set aside in a warm place.

3 In a large bowl, combine the egg yolks, five spice powder, a pinch of white pepper and salt, the honey, rice wine or sherry and Worcestershire sauce. Add the pork, mix well to combine and place in the fridge to marinate for at least 10 minutes, or preferably overnight if time allows.

4 Fill a deep-fat fryer or large pan two-thirds full with vegetable oil and heat to 190°C. Meanwhile, drain the pork thoroughly and pat dry with clean kitchen paper.

5 In a large bowl, lightly whisk the egg whites until thick and foamy (but stop before they start to hold soft peaks). Place the cornflour on a large plate. Dip the pork pieces first into the egg white, then into the cornflour before gently dropping them into the hot oil. Deep-fry in batches, 4-5 pieces at a time, for 2-3 minutes or until golden brown. Put on a plate and keep the fried pieces warm in a low oven if required.

6 Serve the cooked pork in warm bowls or plates, with the sweet 'n' sour sauce and rice.

Wine suggestion
Wines that have a touch of sweetness and plenty of body and fruit flavour are ideal for this - try Viognier or Pinot Gris.

Steamed sea bass with chilli, ginger, garlic & soy sauce

This is a dish that our executive chef orders every time he eats at his local Chinese restaurant – so much so that it has become the proprietor's joke. It's an utterly simple recipe that still delivers a punchy flavour. The key is freshness - from the sea bass right through to the chillies, because each little flavour dances around the dish, playing its part in the overall impression. So, if the sea bass isn't fresh enough on the day, choose bream, salmon or trout instead.

Serves 2

1 sea bass (approx. 500-600g), cleaned and scaled

½ Chinese cabbage, core removed and finely shredded

1 thumb-sized piece fresh root ginger, peeled and cut into matchsticks

4 garlic cloves, peeled and thinly sliced

1 large red chilli, finely sliced into rings, deseeded

½ spring onion, finely sliced

1 tbsp light soy sauce

1 tbsp rice wine vinegar

3 tbsp sesame oil

Small bunch coriander, leaves picked

Small bunch mint, leaves picked

Small bunch basil, leaves picked

Lime wedges, to serve

Prepare 30 minutes
Cook 15-20 minutes

1 Put a flower-petal steamer inside a large wide pan and pour in enough water to come up to just below the steamer. Place over a medium heat and bring to the boil, then turn down to a simmer.

2 Put the Chinese cabbage on to a medium plate that will fit the steamer and lay the fish on top. Scatter with the ginger, garlic and chilli. Place in the steamer and cover with the lid. Cook for 12 minutes. It's ready when the fish easily comes away from the bone - check this using a small prep knife.

3 Meanwhile, mix together the soy sauce and vinegar in a small bowl and set aside.

4 Add the sesame oil to a small pan and heat until fairly hot - don't allow it to smoke.

5 Remove the fish from the steamer and pour off the juices into the bowl with the soy sauce and vinegar. Lift the fish and cabbage on to a large serving dish, taking care not to break the fish, as it's very delicate. Pour over the soy sauce and vinegar, then the hot sesame oil - this should cause it to sizzle. Then sprinkle over the spring onion and herbs, and serve with the lime wedges on the side.

Vegetarian 5

Wild mushroom risotto

We have the Arabs to thank for this, one of Italy's most famous dishes - they introduced rice to Sicily and Spain in the 14th century. Italy now grows it in several regions - in fact, it's so abundant in the Po Valley that risotto is more common there than pasta. The texture should be fluid - not stodgy and not too thin - and, because rice absorbs everything, the quality of the ingredients you use really comes through. Here, the rich nuttiness of wild mushrooms makes a great low-fat substitute for meat.

Serves 4

30g dried mushrooms
150g mixed mushrooms such as
    shiitake (stalks removed), button
    and chestnut, finely sliced
1 litre light vegetable stock
2 tbsp olive oil
40g butter
3 shallots, finely chopped
1 garlic clove, very finely chopped
300g risotto rice
150ml dry white wine
Salt and freshly ground black pepper
50g Parmesan, finely grated, plus
    extra shavings to garnish
Small bunch flat-leafed parsley, finely
    chopped

Prepare 10 minutes
Cook 40-45 minutes

1 Put the dried mushrooms in a small bowl and cover completely with boiling water. Leave to soak for 10 minutes. Drain the juices into a bowl and set aside. Finely chop the mixed mushrooms and set aside. Add the mushroom soaking liquor to the vegetable stock and simmer gently in a saucepan.

2 Heat 1 tbsp of the olive oil in a frying pan and cook the sliced, mixed mushrooms for 2 minutes, or until softened, stirring occasionally. Take off the heat and set aside.

3 Melt half the butter in a large saucepan with a wide base (even a high-sided frying pan or wok) with the remaining olive oil and stir in the shallots. Cook gently for 5 minutes without colouring. Stir in the garlic and cook for 1 minute. Add the soaked mushrooms and continue to cook for another 2 minutes. Stir in the rice and cook for a further 2 minutes. Add the wine and cook until evaporated, stirring occasionally.

4 Gradually add the hot stock, one ladleful at a time, and stir in, allowing each to be absorbed before adding the next. This will take about 20 minutes. Keep a close eye on it now - stir constantly and taste regularly to check the consistency: you want the grains to still have a slight bite, rather than become overcooked and stodgy. Don't forget that it continues to cook in the hot pan after you have removed it from the heat. Season well.

5 Take the pan off the heat and stir in the remaining butter, the Parmesan and parsley, along with most of the reserved cooked mushrooms, leaving a few to garnish the top. Reheat briefly if necessary until piping hot. Divide between four bowls, topping with the remaining mushrooms and some shavings of Parmesan.

> **Wine suggestion**
> This needs a red with a refreshing character to balance the cheese and gentle savoury flavours. Try Burgundy from the Côtes de Nuits, Beaujolais-Villages from one of the more southerly vineyards, or a northern Italian red such as Dolcetto, Barolo or Barbaresco.

Sri Lankan cashew nut curry

Although Sri Lanka's cuisine varies from region to region, what links them is the fact that food is cooked from scratch and revolves around rice served with a variety of curries. This particular recipe achieves a wonderful depth of flavour, with nutrient-packed cashew nuts giving a lovely sweetness. It also works brilliantly with butternut squash or sweet potato.

Serves 4

250g unsalted cashew nuts
4 tbsp groundnut oil (or coconut oil)
8cm stick cinnamon, broken in half
1 large onion, finely chopped
6 garlic cloves, finely chopped
4cm piece fresh root ginger, peeled and finely grated
2 mild green chillies, deseeded and thinly sliced
2 tsp medium curry powder
400ml coconut milk
2 sticks lemongrass, lightly bruised with the back of a knife
4 dried curry leaves
4 kaffir lime leaves
100g green beans, cut in half
Salt and freshly ground black pepper
2 tbsp light brown sugar
Juice of 1 lime
2 tbsp fresh coriander, roughly chopped
2 tbsp fresh basil, leaves picked

Prepare 20 minutes, plus 20 minutes soaking
Cook 30 minutes

1 Put the cashew nuts in a bowl and cover with boiling water. Leave to stand for 20 minutes.

2 Heat the oil in a heavy-based pan and add the cinnamon stick. Fry on a medium heat for 2 minutes until it smells fragrant. Add the onion and fry for 5 minutes more until it starts to turn golden, then tip in the garlic, ginger and chillies and fry for 2 minutes, stirring often.

3 Sprinkle in the curry powder and stir through for 2 minutes on a medium heat. Add the coconut milk, lemongrass, curry leaves and kaffir lime leaves and bring to the boil. Drain the cashew nuts and add them to the curry. Simmer on a medium heat for 10 minutes, then stir in the beans and 100ml water. Simmer for a further 10 minutes. Season to taste.

4 Add the sugar, lime juice, coriander and basil and stir through until the sugar has dissolved. Remove the lemongrass and cinnamon if you wish, then serve.

"To make this a more substantial dish, add cubed squash to the curry at the same stage as the cashew nuts."

James B's tip

Spiced aubergine ragout with panisse & herb yoghurt

Panisse is a fried, chickpea-flour cake from the South of France that is often nibbled as a snack with a glass of wine. Here, however, it's part of a meal. The batter is similar to what you get when you're making polenta, and the finished 'chips' are utterly fantastic alongside this richly delicious ragout. For a lighter version, just switch to reduced-fat yoghurt.

Serves 4

For the ragout:
2 medium onions, finely chopped
2 garlic cloves, crushed
1 tbsp olive oil
Salt and freshly ground black pepper
½ tsp cayenne pepper
2 tsp ground cumin
2 tsp ground coriander
400g can chopped tomatoes
1 large aubergine, diced into 2cm cubes
100g canned chickpeas, drained
1 tbsp red wine vinegar
Pinch sugar
2 tbsp fresh coriander, finely chopped
2 tbsp toasted pine nuts, to garnish

For the panisse:
1 tbsp olive oil
250g chickpea flour (gram flour)
Vegetable oil, for deep-frying

For the herb yoghurt:
150ml Greek yoghurt
2 tbsp fresh mint, finely chopped

Prepare 1 hour
Cook 1 hour, plus 10 minutes cooling

1 To make the ragout, fry the onions and garlic in a pan with the olive oil and a pinch of salt until very soft. Add the cayenne, cumin and coriander and cook for 5 minutes.

2 Stir in the tomatoes, aubergine, chickpeas and vinegar with the sugar and some seasoning. Bring to a gentle boil, then simmer for 30 minutes until the aubergine is tender and the mixture is thick and rich. Stir in the coriander.

3 To make the panisse, preheat a deep-fat fryer to 200°C. Bring 1 litre cold water to the boil in a pan with the olive oil and a pinch of salt. Boil for 2 minutes, then stir in the chickpea flour - the mixture will become very thick. Cook for 10 minutes, stirring continuously.

4 Once cooked, spread the mixture on to a lightly greased baking tray and allow to set. When set, cut into chunky 'chips' (each around 6cm x 2cm) and deep-fry for 5 minutes until crisp and golden.

5 Stir the yoghurt and mint together in a bowl and season.

6 To serve, spoon the ragout into a large bowl and garnish with the crisp chickpea chips. Drizzle over a little herb yoghurt and sprinkle with the toasted pine nuts.

"Add any of your favourite pulses to this stew — puy lentils, borlotti beans or cannellini beans all suit it well. If you like a bit of extra sweetness, throw in a handful of raisins towards the end of the cooking time." **Claire's tip**

Spicy potato curry with paneer, broad beans & pumpkin seeds

This is a great 'use up' dish - you can just throw in whatever vegetables you have lurking in the fridge and contribute handsomely to your five-a-day requirement. Paneer (the fresh cheese you find in South Asian cuisine, particularly Indian) gives it a protein punch that's a healthy addition to vegetarian food.

Serves 4

4 tbsp groundnut oil
1 medium red onion, roughly chopped
300g baby new potatoes, halved
250g paneer cheese, diced
6 curry leaves
4 kaffir lime leaves
1 tsp cumin seeds
3cm piece fresh root ginger, peeled and roughly chopped
8 garlic cloves, roughly chopped
½ tsp turmeric
3 green chillies, deseeded and finely chopped
200g over-ripe plum tomatoes, roughly chopped
150ml vegetable stock
1 tsp garam masala paste (see recipe, right)
½ tsp salt
Freshly ground black pepper
160g frozen broad beans, thawed and shelled
2 tbsp coriander, roughly chopped
40g baby spinach
40g pumpkin seeds

Prepare 45 minutes
Cook 25 minutes

1 Heat a heavy-based pan, add 2 tbsp of the groundnut oil and fry the onion and potatoes for 5 minutes over a high heat. Remove from the pan using a slotted spoon and drain on some kitchen paper.

2 Add another 1 tbsp of the oil to the same pan and fry the paneer over a high heat, turning regularly to make sure it's lightly browned all over. Remove and pat dry on kitchen paper.

3 Add the remaining oil to the pan, turn down the heat and stir in the curry and lime leaves, cumin seeds, ginger and garlic and fry for 1 minute. Stir in the turmeric, chillies, tomatoes, stock, garam masala paste and the salt. Season to taste with the pepper and bring to the boil.

4 Add the potatoes and paneer, cover and simmer for 10 minutes or until the potatoes are soft. Add a little water if the mixture looks dry. Tip in the broad beans, coriander, spinach and some salt and freshly ground black pepper, then simmer for a further 4 minutes. Serve sprinkled with the pumpkin seeds.

Garam masala paste

Don't be tempted to buy ready-made garam masala paste - this one is authentic and will keep in an airtight container in the fridge for up to a fortnight, or in the freezer for up to a month.

Heat a dry, heavy-based frying pan over a medium heat, and add 1 tbsp coriander seeds, 12 whole cloves and 1 tsp cumin seeds and cook until they darken slightly and give off an aromatic fragrance. Tip into a spice grinder or coffee mill, and grind to a powder. Put this mixture together with 2 medium quartered onions; 6 garlic cloves; 50g fresh root ginger; 1 tbsp tamarind purée; 1 tsp ground turmeric; 6 medium hot, deseeded and chopped red chillies; 50ml red wine vinegar; and 60ml creamed coconut into a food processor and blend until smooth.

Artichoke & green olive puff pastry pies

The beauty of these little pies is that you can personalise them. Use any of your favourite ingredients as a filling - for example, leeks instead of shallots, leftover cooked potatoes instead of artichokes and wild mushrooms would be a delicious combination.

Makes 4

20g unsalted butter
4 large shallots, finely sliced
2 garlic cloves, finely minced
8 sprigs thyme, leaves picked and
    finely chopped
5 large sage leaves, finely sliced
Salt and freshly ground black pepper
2 tbsp vermouth
5 large, marinated artichoke hearts,
    roughly chopped
80g green olives, drained, stoned
    and roughly chopped
75ml double cream
400g ready-rolled puff pastry
Plain flour, for rolling out
2 medium egg yolks, beaten, for glazing

Prepare 15 minutes
Cook 35–40 minutes

1 Preheat the oven to 180°C/160°C fan oven/gas mark 4. Melt half the butter in a pan and cook the shallots, garlic, thyme and sage with a pinch of salt until very soft. Add the vermouth and let it bubble until reduced by half.

2 Stir in the artichokes, olives and cream and bring to the boil. Season to taste.

3 Grease four 4cm x 10cm loose-bottomed tartlet cases with the remaining butter. Unroll the pastry on a floured work surface and cut four x 16cm diameter circles to line each case. Fit into each case, then divide the artichoke mixture among them. Using the remaining pastry, cut out 4 circles to cover the pies. Use some of the beaten egg yolk to brush the edge of the pastry. Top each pie with a lid and crimp the edges to seal.

4 Brush the pies with the rest of the beaten egg yolk, then bake for 30 minutes until golden brown and crisp.

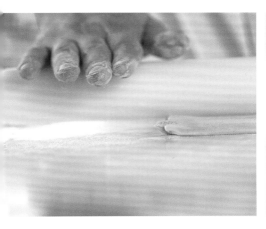

"Shredded basil, mint or parsley folded through the mixture would add freshness to the pie, but you can experiment with any of your favourite herbs, plus even freshly grated zest of a lemon."

Claire's tip

Spanakopitas

These little parcels always remind us of hot summer holidays in Greece. They're ideal for al fresco eating and are just as good eaten cold, which makes them a useful picnic food. You can substitute an unsaturated oil such as rapeseed or sunflower when layering the filo pastry sheets - it won't reduce the calories, but it may help your arteries!

Makes about 20

400g baby leaf spinach
1 tbsp olive oil
1 large onion, diced
2 spring onions, thinly sliced
200g feta, crumbled
2 tbsp ricotta
Small bunch fresh flat-leaf parsley, chopped
3 tbsp fresh dill, chopped
1 medium egg yolk, lightly beaten
Salt and freshly ground black pepper
¼ tsp freshly grated nutmeg
7 sheets (32cm x 40cm) filo pastry
50ml clarified butter (see tip on page 77)

Prepare 10-15 minutes, plus cooling
Cook 15-20 minutes

1 Preheat the oven to 200°C/180°C fan oven/gas mark 6. Put the spinach in a large pan with a drizzle of water. Cover and cook until the spinach has just wilted. Tip into a colander lined with a clean J-cloth. Cool a little, then wrap the cloth around the spinach and squeeze out excess water. Roughly chop the spinach on a board.

2 Heat the oil in a pan and gently fry the diced onion and sliced spring onions for 5-10 minutes until softened. Allow the onions to cool slightly, then mix with the feta, ricotta, spinach, herbs and egg yolk. Once combined, season with salt, pepper and the nutmeg. Place the mixture in the fridge to cool.

3 Taking one sheet of pastry at a time, cut each sheet into 3 strips and brush lightly with the clarified butter. Place 1 dessertspoon of filling slightly off-centre at one end of each strip and fold over the corner next to the filling to form a triangle. Keep folding the pastry, maintaining the triangle, until you reach the end. Brush with more butter and place on a greased baking sheet. Repeat with the remaining filo sheets and filling.

4 Bake for approximately 15-20 minutes until lightly browned. Serve the spanakopitas warm or at room temperature.

"To get ahead, stop after Step 3, transfer to an airtight container and chill between parchment for up to 2 days. When you're ready, preheat the oven, remove from the fridge 30 minutes before to take the chill off them, then bake as per Step 4." **Claire's tip**

Ribollita

This hearty, peasant Tuscan soup is packed with vegetables. In the true Italian tradition where nothing is wasted, it used to be made from leftovers - indeed, 'ribollita' literally means 'reboiled'. Simple, nourishing and delicious.

Serves 6

6 tbsp olive oil
1 red onion, finely chopped
6 garlic cloves, chopped
1 carrot, chopped
2 celery stalks, chopped
½ x 400g can chopped tomatoes
2 litres vegetable stock
1 dried Kashmiri chilli
Large bunch fresh flat-leaf parsley, finely chopped
¼ Savoy cabbage, trimmed and finely shredded
100g spring greens, trimmed and shredded
2 courgettes, trimmed and diced
410g can borlotti beans, drained
Salt and freshly ground black pepper
1 day-old ciabatta loaf
Extra virgin olive oil, to drizzle
Parmesan shavings, to serve

Prepare 30 minutes
Cook 1-1½ hours

1 Heat the oil in a large pan, add the onion, garlic, carrot and celery and cook gently for 30 minutes over a low heat or until soft, stirring occasionally. Stir in the tomatoes, stock and chilli and simmer for a further 30 minutes.

2 Stir in the parsley, green vegetables and borlotti beans, season with salt and freshly ground black pepper and simmer for a further 30 minutes.

3 Remove the crust from the loaf and discard. Tear up the bread and divide between warmed soup bowls. Remove the chilli from the pan, and spoon the soup over the bread.

4 Serve immediately, drizzled with some olive oil and scattered with shavings of Parmesan.

"Don't throw away any leftover Parmesan rind: cut it into cubes and drop them into the soup once you've added the stock – it gives great depth of flavour, plus a touch of creaminess."

Claire's tip

Potato gnocchi with sage butter & Parmesan

These little dumplings are all about texture - they have to be soft, pillowy and inviting. If you try to keep them for more than a couple of hours once they're prepared, they tend to go sticky - even in a fridge. Eat them without sauce ('gnocchi nudi', or 'naked gnocchi') or with tomato sauce, pesto, or just plain butter and cheese.

Serves 4

650g unpeeled floury potatoes
1 tsp salt
110g plain flour, plus extra for dusting
1 medium egg
1 tbsp light olive oil
25g butter
4 sprigs fresh sage, leaves picked
50g Parmesan, freshly grated
Coarsely ground black pepper

Prepare 30 minutes
Cook 40 minutes

1 Peel and chop the potatoes, then put in a pan of cold water with the salt. Cover, bring to the boil and simmer until just tender. Drain well and push through a potato ricer into a large bowl. Mash lightly with a fork and allow to cool to room temperature.

2 Add the flour, egg and a pinch of salt and mash together. Turn out on to a lightly floured surface and knead together very lightly until you have a smooth dough (a little extra flour can be used if it seems too sticky). Divide the mixture into 4 even pieces, then, using your hands, roll 1 piece into a sausage shape about 2cm thick. Cut into 2cm chunks and put on a lightly floured tray. Do the same with the other 3 pieces.

3 Bring a pan of lightly salted water to just below simmering point and add the gnocchi. They will sink at first, then, once they've risen to the surface, poach them at a very gentle simmer for approximately 1 minute until they have cooked through and firmed up. Remove the gnocchi from the water using a slotted spoon and place on a large plate. Allow to cool for 5 minutes.

4 Preheat a non-stick frying pan over a medium heat and add the oil. When hot, add the gnocchi and fry on one side for 2-3 minutes or until golden brown. Turn them over and add the butter and sage leaves. Continue to cook for a further 2-3 minutes or until the gnocchi are browned on both sides and the sage leaves are crisp.

5 Serve on warmed plates with the Parmesan and some coarsely ground black pepper.

"Try experimenting with different flavours by adding fresh herbs, cooked spinach or a salty black olive puree to the gnocchi mixture."

Claire's tip

Spinach & ricotta tortellini

There are a couple of stories that 'explain' the provenance of tortellini. The one we like best is that it was invented in Castelfranco Emilia and owes its shape to Lucrezia Borgia's navel! One night, so the legend goes, she checked into an inn there. The host was so smitten that he couldn't resist peeking into her room through the keyhole. All he could see was her navel, and it was this vision that inspired him to create tortellini!

Serves 2

For the pasta dough:
95g 00 pasta flour, plus extra for
    dusting
1 large egg
1 egg yolk

For the filling:
400g fresh spinach
150g ricotta
3 tbsp finely grated Parmesan
1 medium egg
Nutmeg, freshly grated
Salt and freshly ground black pepper

Prepare 1 hour, plus 45 minutes
    kneading and resting
Cook 3-4 minutes

1 Place the pasta flour in a food processor and, with the motor running, add the egg and the egg yolk. Stop blending when the dough reaches a coarse breadcrumb consistency – don't overwork the dough into a single mass.

2 Remove the coarse crumb mixture from the processor and tip on to a board, then bring together with your hands. Knead for 10-15 minutes until you have a smooth dough – it should be supple and slightly soft, but not sticky. Wrap in cling film and rest in the fridge for at least 30 minutes.

3 To make the filling, put the spinach in a pan with a drizzle of water. Cover and allow to wilt. Drain well, then cool and squeeze out as much water as you can. Put on a board and finely chop. Tip into a bowl and add the ricotta, Parmesan and egg. Mix together until well combined. Season with freshly grated nutmeg and salt and pepper to taste.

4 Roll out the dough with a pasta machine until wafer thin and silky (you might need an extra pair of helping hands at this stage), then cut discs using a 10cm round cutter.

5 Brush a pasta disc with a little cold water and place a small teaspoon of the spinach and ricotta mixture on top (don't overfill). Fold the pasta over the filling to create a semi-circular parcel. Press firmly to seal the edges. Brush one end of the parcel with a little more water, bring the two ends of the parcel together and secure firmly to make a tortellini. Repeat the process with the remaining filling and pasta discs. Put on a tray, lightly dusted with pasta flour, cover loosely with cling film and transfer to the fridge to rest for 5 minutes to set so they maintain their shape.

6 Cook the tortellini in plenty of boiling, salted water for 3-4 minutes or until they have risen to the surface. Drain well and serve immediately with your favourite sauce.

Lemon, apricot, mint & coriander couscous

Couscous is the ambassador of North African cuisine and one of the defining ingredients of Morocco's culinary tradition. It's made from semolina wheat and is a versatile addition to the dry store cupboard, since it can be a main dish, a side dish or even a dessert. This particular recipe is the perfect accompaniment to a slow-cooked tagine.

Serves 6

200g couscous
400ml vegetable stock
2 tbsp olive oil
1 medium onion, finely diced
1 large chilli, deseeded and finely
    chopped
100g dried apricots, roughly
    chopped
60g sultanas
40g preserved lemon, finely chopped
2 tbsp fresh mint, roughly
    chopped
 Small bunch fresh coriander, finely
    chopped
 Juice of 1 lemon
½ tsp salt

Prepare 30 minutes
Cook 10–12 minutes

1 Put the couscous in a bowl. Bring the stock to the boil in a pan, then pour over the couscous. Cover with cling film and leave for 6 minutes.

2 Heat the olive oil in a medium-sized pan and fry the onion and chilli over a medium heat for 4 minutes until the onion has softened slightly.

3 Tip the onion mixture on to a large tray and spoon over the couscous. Add the apricots, sultanas, preserved lemon, mint, coriander, lemon juice and salt and gently fold through with two forks to make a light, fluffy mix. Spoon into a serving dish and serve with Moroccan Slow-cooked Lamb Tagine (see page 169).

Frank Ács is an enthusiastic home cook and has attended cooking classes in several countries. "I reckon that this school is the most interesting, informative, creative, exciting, and just plain fun, of them all!"

Fish & shellfish 6

Linguine with crab, garlic, chilli & basil

Sweet crab meat with a touch of heat combined with the freshness of the lemon cutting through it is gastronomic heaven - and with its preparation and cooking time, it certainly qualifies as food in a flash.

Serves 4

500g dried linguine
200g brown crab meat
Squeeze lemon juice
Salt and freshly ground black pepper
50g butter, melted
2 tbsp olive oil
4 garlic cloves, finely chopped
1 red chilli, deseeded and finely
   chopped
300g white crab meat
Small bunch basil

Prepare 10 minutes
Cook 10 minutes

1 Bring a large pan of salted water to the boil and add the linguine, making sure it's all immersed in the water and starting to soften. Cook for 8-9 minutes, or according to the packet instructions, until al dente.

2 Meanwhile, place the brown crab meat in a blender with the lemon juice. Season well with salt and black pepper. With the motor running, gradually add the melted butter through the funnel to make a thick-ish sauce. Remove and set aside.

3 Just before the pasta is ready, heat the oil in a large saucepan and gently cook the garlic and chilli until softened without colouring. When the linguine is cooked, drain in a colander, leaving some of the cooking water in the pan - you may need this later.

4 Add the pasta to the garlic and chilli oil mixture and turn to coat, then mix in the brown crab meat to achieve a creamy consistency. Fold in the white crab meat, making sure it's well distributed through the pasta. Toss the pasta thoroughly, adding some extra cooking water if it becomes too dry. Chop the basil coarsely and sprinkle in. Season to taste and serve.

"The trick is to drain the linguine when it's al dente so that it doesn't overcook as you add the crab and the flavourings. Make sure the linguine is well seasoned and deliciously slippery. The amount of chilli, needless to say, is up to you. I like plenty."

Claire's tip

Cullen skink

This smoked haddock and potato soup hails from the fishing village of Cullen in Morayshire, northeast Scotland. 'Skink' actually means 'shin', because at one time it was made from shin of beef, but age has a way of blurring original intentions, and over the years it morphed into a soup whose main ingredient is smoked haddock. Very warming and tasty it is, too.

Serves 4

340g undyed smoked haddock fillets
285ml milk
1 onion, halved: one half sliced and the other finely chopped
1 small blade mace
30g butter
225g potatoes, peeled and chopped into 1cm pieces
1 tomato, peeled, deseeded and diced
1 tbsp fresh curly parsley, finely chopped
2 tbsp double cream (optional)

Prepare 15 minutes
Cook 40 minutes

1 Lay the smoked haddock skin side up in a large saucepan. Pour over the milk with 285ml water and add the sliced onion and mace. Cover with the lid and place over a medium heat to poach for 5 minutes. Take off the heat and leave to stand for 10 minutes.

2 Meanwhile, melt the butter in a large saucepan, add the finely chopped onion and potatoes and cook very slowly over a low heat for 15-20 minutes until soft.

3 Remove the fish from the poaching liquid, discard the skin and any bones, flake into bite-sized pieces and set aside. Strain the cooking liquid on to the onion and potato mixture and simmer for a further 5 minutes.

4 Purée the soup with a hand blender or in a food processor (you could also push the soup through a sieve for a finer result) and return to a clean pan.

5 Reheat the soup gently and add the flaked fish, tomato and parsley. Season with salt and pepper and serve immediately, drizzled with the cream (if using).

"For a more luxurious version, try serving this soup with a soft poached egg floating on top."

Gordon's tip

Thai red seafood curry

It sometimes surprises Westerners to discover that Thailand has around 40 different ethnic groups, each with their own culture and language. But one characteristic they all strive for is balance. Each dish, or overall meal, should reflect the five taste senses: hot (spicy), sour, sweet, salty and bitter, obtained from a wide variety of ingredients, all prepared with a light touch.

Serves 6

For the red Thai curry paste:

5 red chillies, deseeded and finely chopped
5 shallots, finely chopped
8cm piece fresh root ginger, chopped
5 garlic cloves, chopped
2 lemongrass sticks, chopped
½ tbsp Thai fish paste
4 tbsp sunflower oil
½ tsp turmeric
1 tsp ground coriander
½ tsp ground cumin
1 tsp paprika
Zest of 1 lime

For the curry:

1 cooked lobster, weight about 400g
200g prepared baby squid
250g bream, cut into 6cm pieces
12 large, raw, unshelled prawns
24 large, live mussels, cleaned
3 tbsp sunflower oil
500ml chicken stock
400ml coconut milk
3 tbsp Thai fish sauce
2 limes
3 fresh or 4 dried kaffir lime leaves (optional)
Small bunch fresh basil, roughly torn

Prepare 30 minutes
Cook 20-25 minutes

1 First make the paste: place all the ingredients into a food processor with 2 tbsp cold water and blend until smooth. Remove and set aside.

2 Pull the claws off the lobster, break each one into three and lightly crack the shells with a rolling pin. Detach the head and legs from the tail section and discard the head. Cut the tail section through the shell into 3 even-sized pieces.

3 Remove the tentacles from the squid. Slice the squid in half lengthways and place with the bream, prawns and cleaned mussels.

4 To make the curry, heat the oil in a large saucepan and add the red curry paste. Fry for 2 minutes or until the paste starts to separate from the oil slightly. Add the stock, coconut milk and Thai fish sauce, and heat gently.

5 Meanwhile, juice and zest the limes. Add the zest to the pan with the kaffir lime leaves (if using) and gently simmer everything together for 10 minutes.

6 Add the lobster to the pan and simmer for 2 minutes, then stir in the squid, bream, prawns and mussels and cook for a further 5 minutes or until the mussels have completely opened. Discard any that remain closed. Stir in the basil and lime juice. Check for seasoning.

7 Transfer everything to a large, shallow platter and scatter over with the crispy shallot and the chilli garnishes (see below), and serve with Thai jasmine rice.

Chilli and shallot garnishes

For the chilli garnish, mix 4 medium-sized, deseeded and thinly sliced red chillies with 50ml rice wine vinegar in a small bowl. Set aside. For the crispy shallot garnish, heat 1 litre sunflower oil in a deep-fat fryer to 180°C and add 4 thinly sliced shallots, 6 thinly sliced garlic cloves and 50g halved cashew nuts, and fry until crisp and golden brown. Take care not to overcook the garlic or it will taste bitter. Lift out with a slotted spoon and place on a plate lined with kitchen paper to drain, season with a little salt and set aside until ready to use. Drain the vinegar from the chillies, ready to use to garnish.

Crisp-fried sea bass in sweet chilli sauce, with mango & mint salad

This dish is what epitomises the Thai philosophy - hot, sour, salty, sweet: beautifully fresh, crispy fish served with chilli heat, mango sweetness, Thai fish sauce saltiness, and the sourness of fresh lime juice squeezed over. It's also magnificent with bream, mackerel, or any other round fish.

Serves 4

2 whole sea bass, bream or gurnard, scaled (about 350g each)
30g cornflour
½ tsp sea salt
Pinch dried chilli flakes
1 litre sunflower oil, for deep-frying

For the chilli sauce:
100ml white wine vinegar
60g palm sugar or light muscovado sugar
1 red chilli, deseeded and very finely chopped
1 tbsp tamarind paste
2 tsp Thai fish sauce

For the crispy garlic and shallots:
60g shallots, thinly sliced
4 garlic cloves, thinly sliced

For the mango and mint salad:
2 ripe mangoes, peeled, stone removed and cut into large chunks
2 tbsp fresh mint, leaves picked
2 tbsp Thai holy basil (use regular basil if not available)
2 tbsp coriander leaves
1 red chilli, deseeded and cut into thin strips
1 carrot, cut into thin strips using a potato peeler
Juice of 1 lime

Prepare 40 minutes
Cook 20 minutes

1 First make the chilli sauce: put the vinegar, sugar and chilli into a small pan and bring to the boil. Simmer for 6 minutes, then remove and add the tamarind paste and fish sauce. The sauce should be a thick, sticky consistency. Set aside and keep warm.

2 Fillet the sea bass (see our step-by-step instructions on pages 24-25) to make 4 fillets from the 2 fish. Put the cornflour in a shallow dish and stir in the salt and dried chilli flakes, and gently coat the sea bass fillets in this mix.

3 Pour 1 litre sunflower oil into a large wok or fryer, and heat to 180°C. You can test when the oil is ready by dropping in a small piece of vegetable - if it sizzles, it's ready. Slide the fish into the oil and fry for 6 minutes or until golden brown and crisp. Lift out with a slotted spoon and place on a plate lined with kitchen paper to drain.

4 Make the crispy shallots and garlic: add the shallots to the oil and fry for 1 minute, then add the garlic and fry for 30 seconds or until it starts to turn light brown. Don't let it go too dark or it'll taste bitter. Lift on to kitchen paper and drain. Set aside.

5 For the mango and mint salad, toss all the ingredients together in a bowl and season to taste.

6 Divide the salad between four plates, top with the fish, crispy shallots and garlic, then spoon over the chilli sauce. Serve immediately.

"This also works well with sea bream and tilapia. For a healthier alternative, try coating the fish with 1 tbsp oil and then grilling or pan-frying instead of deep-frying."

Jon's tip

Moules marinière

This translates as 'sailor's mussels' and is a hugely popular French classic. Make sure the mussels are really fresh - the best way to eat them is to use an empty mussel shell as a tool to pick the other mussels from their shells. Serve with big chunks of bread to sop up all those wonderful juices at the bottom of the bowl. Bon appétit!

Serves 4

2kg mussels
50g unsalted butter
1 medium onion, finely chopped
2 garlic cloves, finely minced
1 celery stick, finely chopped
Salt and freshly ground black pepper
200ml white wine
3 tbsp whipping cream
Small bunch flat-leaf parsley, finely
   chopped

Prepare 20 minutes
Cook 10 minutes

1 Wash the mussels well, removing any beards and discarding any shells that are damaged or remain open when tapped.

2 Melt the butter in a large pan over a medium heat, then sweat the onion, garlic and celery until very soft. Do not colour the onion. Season with a little salt.

3 Add the mussels, white wine and a splash of water. Cover and cook over a high heat for 5-6 minutes, or until all the mussels have opened. Discard any that remain closed.

4 Stir in the cream and parsley, season with black pepper, then divide among four large warmed bowls.

"Try adding some fresh tomato and basil for a Provencale version of this dish, but leave out the cream."

James B's tip

"When you're about to fry the fish, don't just drop it straight into the oil. Start off by suspending it vertically so that about an inch of the fish is below the surface of the oil for 10 seconds. This prevents the fish from sticking to the bottom of the fryer!" **Gordon's tip**

Beer-battered cod with tartare sauce & chips

Who would have thought that, 151 years after the first fish and chip shop opened in London, this national favourite would still occupy pole position? It works just as well with pollock, hake or skate, but whichever you choose, it's all about the freshness of the fish and the crispiness of the batter.

Serves 4

900g Maris Piper potatoes, cut lengthways into 1cm thick chips
1-2 litres sunflower or vegetable oil
125g self-raising flour
100ml soda water
100ml light beer, such as Becks
Plain flour, for dusting
Salt and freshly ground black pepper
4 x 175g pieces cod loin

For the tartare sauce:
200g good-quality mayonnaise
8 finely chopped green olives
6 finely chopped gherkins
1 tsp finely chopped capers
2 tsp finely chopped chives
2 tsp finely chopped curly parsley

Prepare 40 minutes
Cook 30 minutes

1 Mix together in a bowl all the ingredients for the tartare sauce and season to taste. Place in the fridge until you're ready to serve.

2 For the chips, preheat the oven to 130°C/110°C fan oven/gas mark ½, and preheat the oil in a deep-fryer to 140°C. First cook them in boiling water until soft, but still whole. Remove from the water, drain on clean, dry kitchen paper and allow to cool. Fry in the oil for about 5 minutes until lightly golden brown, then remove and drain on kitchen paper. Increase the temperature of the oil to 190°C and repeat the frying process until the chips are crisp and a deeper golden brown. Remove from the oil and drain on a plate lined with kitchen paper. Season with salt and transfer the plate to the oven to keep warm.

3 Make the batter by mixing the self-raising flour, soda water and light beer together in a large bowl until smooth. It should be the consistency of double cream.

4 Put a couple of tablespoons of plain flour in a shallow bowl and season it with salt and pepper. Line a board with kitchen paper. Dip the cod into the flour to coat, then dip in the batter. Fry two pieces of fish at a time for 7–8 minutes, until crisp and deep golden brown. Lift on to the kitchen towel to drain. Serve the fish and chips with the tartare sauce on the side.

Oriental tuna salad with avocado, radish & shallot

While we Brits eat more tinned tuna than most other types of fish, it just doesn't compare with the wonderfully meaty flavour and firm, dense texture of fresh tuna. It's also rich in omega-3, the fatty acid essential for good skin and brain function, and a great source of protein. The radishes give a peppery touch and the shallots, a lovely bittersweet crunch.

Serves 2

2 x 150g fresh tuna steaks
   (sustainably sourced)
1 tbsp vegetable oil
Salt and freshly ground black pepper

For the salad:
Vegetable oil, for deep-frying
2 banana shallots, thinly sliced
1 tsp cornflour
Pinch salt
Pinch caster sugar
12 radishes, topped and tailed
½ cucumber, peeled
1 large avocado
2 large handfuls crisp mixed salad
   leaves

For the oriental dressing:
4 tbsp Japanese soy sauce
4 tbsp mirin
2 tbsp toasted sesame oil
1 ball stem ginger in syrup
Juice of 1 lime
Small bunch fresh coriander leaves

Prepare 30 minutes
Cook 20 minutes

1 First make the oriental dressing: combine all the ingredients, except the coriander, in a blender, and blitz to emulsify. Finely slice the coriander and add to the dressing.

2 To make the salad, heat the vegetable oil in a deep-fat fryer to 150°C. Toss the shallots in the cornflour in a bowl, then fry until crisp, golden and caramelised. Lift out with a slotted spoon and drain on a plate lined with kitchen paper. Season with salt and sugar.

3 Use a sharp knife or mandolin to thinly slice the radishes and cucumber into rounds. Halve and stone the avocado, then carefully remove the skin. Thinly slice each half.

4 Preheat a non-stick pan over a medium heat. Brush the tuna with the vegetable oil and season with salt and pepper. Add the tuna to the hot pan, searing for approximately 1-2 minutes on each side, cooking the fish until slightly pink in the centre and keeping it deliciously juicy. Use a sharp knife to carve the tuna across the grain into thin slices.

5 Arrange the thinly sliced vegetables and salad leaves in a shallow salad bowl. Spoon over a little dressing and toss to coat. Place the sliced tuna on top of the salad, then drizzle with a little more dressing. Scatter over the crisp fried shallots and serve.

"The salad works equally well with chargrilled salmon and mackerel. For a spicy oriental dressing, add 1 deseeded and chopped red chilli when you stir in the coriander."

Gordon's tip

Saffron seafood paella

'La paella' is actually the name of the wide, circular pan in which it's made, and which has now become shorthand for the dish itself. It comes from Valencia, where it used to be eaten by Spanish labourers. In those days, it largely featured snails and rabbit, as these could be found in the hills for free. Only the better-off ate chicken and duck - seafood didn't enter the equation at all!

Serves 6

2 tbsp olive oil
1 large onion, finely chopped
6 skinless, boneless chicken thighs, diced
2 garlic cloves, finely chopped
1 large pinch saffron
½ tsp paprika
3 large ripe vine tomatoes, peeled and chopped
500g paella rice
300ml dry white wine
1 litre fish stock
2 monkfish fillets, or any firm white fish fillets, about 200g each, cut into large chunks
50g peas
1 pint mussels in the shell
300g cooked and peeled king prawns
100g flame-roasted peppers, cut into strips
Large bunch fresh flat-leaf parsley, roughly chopped
1 lemon, cut into 6 wedges

Prepare 15 minutes
Cook 35 minutes

1 Heat the olive oil in a wide, shallow pan or paella pan and fry the onion for 2-3 minutes, until starting to soften. Increase the heat to high, add the chicken and brown, then stir in the garlic, saffron and paprika and cook for 2-3 minutes.

2 Stir in the chopped tomatoes, then gently simmer for 8-10 minutes until the tomatoes have softened. Stir in the rice, coating well with the spice and tomato mix.

3 Add the white wine and allow to bubble and reduce by about half before adding all the fish stock. Simmer gently for 15 minutes, or until almost all of the stock has been absorbed. Add the monkfish and leave on a gentle heat for 5 minutes, or until the fish is cooked through and opaque.

4 Add the peas, then the mussels, prawns and pepper strips to the dish, and continue to cook until the mussels open up. Sprinkle over the parsley, dot with lemon wedges, season and serve immediately with a crisp salad.

"Chorizo cooking sausage would make an ideal addition to this classic recipe. Roughly chop a packet of cooking chorizo and add at the beginning with the oil and onion."

Gordon's tip

Moroccan fish tagine

A tagine is a traditional Moroccan stew, but it's also the name of the pot in which it's cooked, which used to be used by the nomads as a portable oven. It's made from heavy, glazed earthenware that holds the heat and moisture well, with a cone-shaped lid that enables it to perform like an oven. You can use a casserole dish, though – just make sure the lid fits well.

Serves 4

3 tbsp olive oil
2 celery sticks, finely chopped
1 carrot, finely chopped
1 small onion, finely chopped
1 small preserved lemon, finely chopped
4 plum tomatoes, finely chopped
600ml fish stock
8 small new potatoes, cut into quarters
8 bream fillets, skin on
8 pitted black Kalamata olives, drained and halved
1 tsp finely chopped fresh coriander
1 tsp finely chopped fresh mint

For the chermoula:

2 tbsp fresh coriander, roughly chopped
3 garlic cloves, roughly chopped
1½ tsp ground cumin
1 tsp salt
½ red chilli, halved, deseeded and roughly chopped
½ tsp saffron strands
4 tbsp extra virgin olive oil
Juice of 1 lemon
1½ tsp paprika

Prepare 20 minutes
Cook 50 minutes

1 First make the chermoula: place all the ingredients into a food processor and blend until smooth. Set aside.

2 Heat 2 tbsp of the olive oil in a large pan, add the celery, carrot and onion and fry gently for 5 minutes, until softened but not browned.

3 Add half the preserved lemon, 2 tbsp of the chermoula, the tomatoes and the stock. Bring to the boil and simmer for 30 minutes.

4 Add the potatoes and simmer for 10 minutes more, until they are tender.

5 For the fish, preheat the grill to high and brush the fillets with the remaining olive oil, season with salt and pepper and cut each one diagonally in half. Grill skin side up for about 6 minutes, until the flesh is opaque and just cooked.

6 Stir the olives, the rest of the chermoula and the remaining preserved lemon into the sauce and check the seasoning. Divide between four bowls, top each with pieces of fish and sprinkle with the chopped coriander and mint.

Seared squid, chorizo & tomato stew

For this dish we use small frozen squid, which are not only very tasty, but they add a terrific visual element to the dish. You can use larger squid rings if you like, but just remember that if you overcook them they'll become tough. If you're not a fan of squid of any sort, try replacing it with large fresh prawns.

Serves 4

5 tbsp olive oil
450g small whole squid
1 large onion, finely chopped
2 garlic cloves, finely chopped
Large pinch smoked paprika
5 sprigs thyme
Zest of ½ lemon
400g canned chopped tomatoes
Salt and freshly ground black pepper
220g cooking chorizo, finely sliced
Small bunch parsley, finely chopped

Prepare 30 minutes
Cook 40 minutes

1 Heat 3 tbsp of the olive oil in a large, heavy-based frying pan and cook the squid in four separate batches. This is important, as overloading the squid can make it steam, whereas we want it to develop a lovely colour. Transfer each cooked portion to a plate while you cook the next batch.

2 When all the squid is cooked, lower the heat under the pan and add the onion and garlic with the rest of the olive oil. Gently sauté until very soft (about 5-6 minutes) then stir in the paprika and continue to fry for 3 minutes. Add the thyme, lemon zest and chopped tomatoes. Season to taste and bring to the boil, then turn down and allow to gently simmer. You need to reduce the sauce by about a third.

3 Preheat the grill to medium-high. Put the chorizo on a lipped baking sheet and grill for 2 minutes or until the fat begins to ooze out. Flip over and grill for another minute or two until golden. Add to the tomato stew with 150ml water. Continue to cook over a low heat for about 10 minutes until the sauce begins to thicken. Taste the sauce at this point to see if it needs seasoning - it should have a rich, deep flavour and the chorizo should come through.

4 Remove the thyme sprigs from the sauce, stir in the squid and parsley and serve immediately.

Steamed brill, mussels, cockles & clams with lemon butter

You can smell and taste the sea from this dish - it's a reminder of the best kind of beach holiday. There's simply no better way to cook and serve seafood than this.

Serves 2

1 whole brill or lemon sole (about 350g)
Salt and freshly ground black pepper

For the lemon butter:
1 large garlic clove
100g unsalted butter, softened
2 tsp lemon juice
1 tsp brandy
Small bunch fresh parsley, chopped

For the sauce:
2-3 shallots, very finely chopped
1 celery stick, very finely chopped
200g mussels, cleaned and picked over
200g clams
100g cockles (optional)
100ml dry white wine
50ml fish stock
1 carrot, very finely chopped
½ leek, very finely chopped

Prepare 30 minutes
Cook 12 minutes

> ### Wine suggestion
> The fish and lemony butter are a good match for a classic cool-climate Chardonnay. Try a Chablis or, for a value option, an Italian white made from Fiano, Grillo or Trebbiano.

1 Fillet the brill on a board into 4 pieces (see pages 26-27) and put on a plate, then season with salt and pepper to taste and roll up. Skewer with a cocktail stick to keep the shape. Quarter-fill a wok with water and bring to the boil. Place a steamer petal inside, or use a steamer if you've got one.

2 To make the lemon butter, put all the ingredients into a blender and whiz to make a coarse paste. Line a small board with cling film, spoon the butter on top, then wrap up. Roll the cling film parcel to shape into a long sausage. Refrigerate for up to a week or freeze for up to one month.

3 Heat a pan with the lid on so that it gets very hot. Add the shallots, celery, mussels, clams and cockles. Then add the white wine and replace the lid. Steam for 1 minute 40 seconds (this sounds very precise, but it prevents undercooking) or until the shellfish is fully open. If any of the shellfish remain unopened, throw them away.

4 Pour the shellfish and liquid into a colander resting over a bowl to reserve the juices. Pour the juices back into the pot and add the fish stock, carrot and leek. Bring to the boil and reduce by half.

5 Meanwhile pick most of the mussels, cockles and clams from their shells, but keep a few intact for garnishing. Set aside.

6 Carefully place the fish on the plate into the steamer petal in the wok and steam for 8 minutes. Remove and pour the cooking water into the sauce.

7 Remove the butter from the fridge, unwrap and thinly slice. Add about 40g of the butter to the sauce in the pan and give it a good whisk. Add the shellfish back into the pan and stir.

8 Put the fish in the centre of a warm plate and spoon over the shellfish mixture, then garnish with reserved, intact shellfish. Serve with spinach.

Maryland crab cakes with tomato, tarragon & chilli salsa

Crab cakes are usually associated with the Chesapeake Bay area - in particular the state of Maryland and the city of Baltimore. The two most common versions of this dish are the street version, called 'Boardwalk' (breaded and deep-fried, served on a burger bun) and the 'Restaurant' (more of a gourmet experience, served on a platter or as an open sandwich). Either way, it makes for a terrific casual supper or lunch.

Serves 4

40g cream crackers
450g fresh white crab meat
2 tbsp freshly chopped parsley
¼ tsp cayenne pepper
1 medium egg, beaten
2 tbsp mayonnaise
1 tbsp English mustard powder
1 tbsp lemon juice
Dash Worcestershire sauce
Pinch salt
4 tbsp clarified butter (see tip on page 77)
Freshly ground white pepper
1 lemon, cut into wedges, to serve

For the salsa:

100g baby tomatoes, roughly diced
½ red onion, finely chopped
1 tbsp extra virgin olive oil
1 tsp tarragon, freshly chopped
Pinch dried chipotle chilli
¼ tsp ground cumin
¼ tsp ground coriander
Salt and freshly ground black pepper

Prepare 40 minutes
Cook 20 minutes

1 Put the crackers in a plastic bag and crush to fine crumbs with a rolling pin. Put the crab meat into a bowl with the parsley and cayenne pepper, and add just enough cracker crumbs to absorb any moisture from the crab (you may not need it all).

2 Whisk the beaten egg in a small bowl with the mayonnaise, mustard powder, lemon juice and Worcestershire sauce, and season with salt. Fold this mix into the crab, but don't break up the lumps of crab too much - you want some texture to come through. Shape the mixture into 8 patties, put them on a plate, cover with cling film and chill for at least 1 hour.

3 Heat the clarified butter in a large frying pan and fry the crab cakes in batches over a medium heat for 3-4 minutes each side until crisp and golden. Keep the first lot warm in the oven while you cook the second batch.

4 To make the salsa, put all the ingredients in a bowl and mix thoroughly. Season to taste. Divide the salsa among four plates and place 2 crab cakes to the side of the salsa. Serve each with a wedge of lemon.

Meat 7

Moroccan slow-cooked lamb tagine

This Berber stew used to be cooked for a very long time in a conical clay pot that allowed the steam to rise and drip back into the mixture. The finished dish was so moist, succulent and healthy that it's no wonder the word got round. The prunes add fibre, plus a whole range of vitamins and minerals, and the tomatoes raise the vitamin C content. Best of all, you just dump everything in the pot and let it cook itself.

Serves 4

2 tbsp olive oil
50g butter
2 large onions, finely diced
4 garlic cloves, crushed
Salt
500g neck or shoulder of lamb, diced
1 tsp paprika
1 tsp ground cumin
1 tsp ground ginger
1 tsp ground coriander
1 large cinnamon stick
½ tsp hot chilli powder
Pinch saffron
2 tsp clear honey
400ml lamb stock
1 x 400g can chopped tomatoes
4 strips orange zest
16 prunes, stoned, but left whole
2 tbsp flaked almonds, toasted
Small bunch fresh coriander, roughly chopped

Prepare 45 minutes
Cook 2-3 hours

1 Heat the oil and butter in a pan and fry the onions and garlic with a pinch of salt until softened.

2 Add the lamb and brown lightly, turning regularly, then add the paprika, cumin, ginger, coriander, cinnamon stick and chilli powder. Cook, stirring continuously, for 2 minutes.

3 Add the saffron, honey, stock, tomatoes and orange zest and bring to the boil. Cover and cook over a very low heat for around 2 hours, until the meat is very tender and the liquid has reduced to a thick sauce. You can add a little water during the cooking process if the mixture seems too dry. Add the prunes for the final 15 minutes of cooking.

4 Scatter the almonds and coriander over the tagine and serve with Lemon, Apricot, Mint & Coriander Couscous (see page 138).

> **Wine suggestion**
> Chilean Carmenère or New Zealand Merlot - the combination of sweetness and spice in this lamb tagine lends itself to New World reds with plenty of fruit and soft texture.

Steak & Guinness pie

This is a hearty dish that partners two of Ireland's greatest assets, beef and Guinness, to fantastic effect, making use of a forgotten cut of meat – the ox cheek. The alcohol tenderises it, producing a wonderfully rich flavour. It's simple to make, big on robust flavours and warms the cockles in winter.

Serves 6

1kg ox cheeks, cut into large cubes
300ml Guinness
150ml full-bodied red wine
2 bay leaves
4 sprigs dried thyme
2 tbsp plain flour, plus extra for rolling out

Salt and freshly ground black pepper
3 tbsp vegetable oil
100g smoked bacon lardons
2 onions, roughly chopped
1 tbsp tomato purée
1 tbsp Worcestershire sauce
250g chestnut mushrooms, quartered

10g unsalted butter
400g all-butter puff pastry
1 medium egg, beaten

Prepare 45 minutes, plus marinating
Cook 3–4 hours

1 Marinate the ox cheeks in a bowl with the Guinness and wine together with the herbs. Place in the fridge for 20 minutes while you prepare the rest of the ingredients.

2 Drain the meat (reserving the marinade), then sprinkle over the flour and a little seasoning to lightly coat the surface of the meat.

3 Heat 1 tbsp of the oil in a pan and brown half the ox cheeks. Transfer to a plate. Add a further tbsp of oil to the pan and brown the other half.

4 Heat the remaining oil in a flameproof casserole and cook the lardons over a high heat for 5 minutes to brown. Add the onions and cook for a further 5 minutes. Stir in the browned ox cheeks, reserved marinade and herbs, tomato purée and Worcestershire sauce. Season, then cover and simmer on the lowest heat for 2½ hours, stirring

occasionally, until the meat is tender. Remove the bay leaves and thyme sprigs and leave to cool.

5 Preheat the oven to 200°C/180°C fan oven/gas mark 6. Fry the mushrooms in the butter in a pan over a high heat for 4 minutes until starting to soften and turn golden. Stir into the stew, then spoon the mixture into a 20cm x 30cm pie dish.

6 On a floured surface, roll the pastry out so that it's a little larger than the dish. Top the pie with the pastry and cut a cross in it. Trim away the excess and press down around the edges. Brush with the beaten egg.

7 Bake for 45 minutes, until the pastry is golden and puffed and the gravy bubbles at the edges. Let it stand for 5 minutes before serving.

Osso bucco with risotto alla Milanese

'Osso bucco' is Italian for 'hollow bone' – the name conjures up visions of guests gnawing right down to the bone to get at the marrow's tasty goodness. This recipe uses tender veal shanks and faithfully follows tradition by pairing it with risotto alla Milanese, an exquisitely creamy rice dish perfumed with saffron and finished with Parmesan and butter. Nothing, but nothing, beats it on a cold winter's night.

Serves 4

2 tbsp olive oil
2 x 200g pieces veal shin (ask the butcher to cut osso bucco style)
1 large onion, finely chopped
1 large carrot, finely chopped
2 garlic cloves, finely chopped
1 tsp plain flour
1 tsp tomato purée
400g can chopped tomatoes
100ml white wine
150ml beef stock
Bouquet garni

For the risotto:
800ml chicken stock
50g unsalted butter
1 large onion, finely chopped
200g risotto rice, such as arborio
75ml dry white wine
10 saffron strands
30g Parmesan, finely grated

For the gremolata:
Finely grated zest of 1 lemon
1 garlic clove, finely chopped
Small bunch fresh flat-leaf parsley, finely chopped

Prepare 1 hour
Cook 1-2 hours

1 Heat half the oil in a frying pan and brown the veal. Heat the remaining oil in a large saucepan and cook the onion, carrot and garlic for a few minutes until softened.

2 Add the flour to the vegetables and stir well to combine, then add the tomato purée, tomatoes, wine and stock. Bring to the boil and add the veal to the pot along with the bouquet garni. Cover and simmer gently for 1-2 hours or until the veal is very tender.

3 Once cooked, remove the veal from the pan and reduce the cooking liquor by half or until thickened and syrupy.

4 Around 30-40 minutes before the end of the veal cooking time, start making the risotto. Put the stock into a pan and bring to a gentle simmer. Melt 40g of the butter in another pan and gently fry the onion until soft. Add the rice, wine and saffron and cook for about 3 minutes, stirring gently and continuously, until the wine has been absorbed.

5 Using a ladle, add the stock a ladleful at a time, stirring constantly, allowing it to be absorbed after each addition. Keep stirring, adding stock little by little until the rice is cooked but still retains bite (about 15-20 minutes).

6 Remove the pan from the heat and add the remaining butter and Parmesan. Stir to combine. Allow the risotto to stand for 3 minutes before serving.

7 Mix together the ingredients for the gremolata and set aside. Divide the risotto between four plates and serve the braised veal with its thick tomato sauce on the side. Sprinkle over some of the gremolata and serve.

Wine suggestion
What's needed here is a refreshing edge, yet still with intensity and richness, to match the Parmesan in the risotto and cut through the density of the dish. So try Amarone or Barolo. You won't go wrong with bigger styles of Dolcetto, either - choose a rich red from Piemonte (Piedmont).

174

Meat

Toad in the hole

The name of this much-loved English dish has baffled people for years, but it has been suggested that it resembles toads hiding in the entrance to burrows, ready to pounce on passing insects. Do we believe this? Do we care? It's a nostalgic dish that everyone's granny has made at one time or another, and it unfailingly makes us smile.

Serves 4

1 tbsp sunflower oil
8 pork sausages

For the batter:
225g plain flour
½ tsp salt
4 eggs
300ml whole milk

Prepare 10 minutes
Cook 35 minutes

1 Preheat the oven to 200°C/180°C fan oven/gas mark 6. Heat the oil in a large ovenproof frying pan over a medium heat, then add the sausages and cook until golden brown all over and cooked through. This will take around 15 minutes. Drain off any excess fat.

2 Meanwhile, make the batter: sift the flour and salt into a bowl, then make a well in the centre, break in the eggs and beat well using a balloon whisk.

3 Gradually beat in the milk to make a smooth, lump-free batter — the consistency should be like double cream.

4 When the sausages are cooked, pour over enough batter to come halfway up the sides of the sausages. Place the pan in the oven for around 15 minutes, or until the batter is puffed up and golden brown. Serve immediately with Caramelised Onion Gravy (see page 41).

"For a light and crisp finished result, make sure your frying pan is very hot before you add the batter."

Claire's tip

Kleftiko

'Kleftiko' is Greek for 'stolen meat', a name that was apparently given to a dish invented by Greek bandits. When they were hungry, they'd dig a hole and line it with hot coals, then lower a stolen lamb into it to cook, leaving it, covered over and undetected, for 24 hours. This version is stunning - the lamb ends up so succulent that the meat just falls off the bone.

Serves 4

1 half shoulder of lamb
Salt and freshly ground black pepper
1 onion, sliced
1 carrot, sliced
2 celery sticks, sliced
2 garlic cloves, roughly chopped
2 tsp dried oregano
2 bay leaves
2 sprigs fresh rosemary
300ml white wine
Small bunch fresh flat-leaf parsley,
    roughly chopped
400g can chopped tomatoes
500g new potatoes, peeled
3 tbsp extra virgin olive oil

Prepare 30 minutes
Cook 3-4 hours

1 Preheat the oven to 180°C/160°C fan oven/gas mark 4. Season the lamb and place in a large casserole dish or roasting tin. Add all the remaining ingredients except the oil, and pour over 600ml cold water. Drizzle over the oil and season well.

2 Cover with foil and place in the oven to cook for 2 hours. You might need to add a little extra water during cooking if the mixture looks a bit dry.

3 After 2 hours, remove the foil and increase the temperature to 200°C/180°C fan oven/gas mark 6 and cook for a further 15 minutes or until the top begins to crisp and brown.

4 Remove the meat from the dish. Stir the vegetables and juices together, and serve with the lamb.

Barbecued spare ribs

Was there ever a more popular export from the American South than the humble barbecue? This cooking method dates back to before the Civil War, and has since been universally adopted. Inexpensive, wonderfully tender and succulent spare ribs are quick and easy to prepare, and great for feeding large numbers of people.

Serves 4

1kg pork spare ribs
6 tbsp balsamic vinegar
6 tbsp tomato ketchup
6 tbsp soy sauce
6 tbsp clear honey
3 tbsp chipotle chilli paste

Prepare 45 minutes
Cook 1½ hours

1 Preheat the oven to 150°C/130°C fan oven/gas mark 2. Place the ribs in a pan of cold water, bring to the boil and skim off any impurities that come to the surface. Turn down to a low heat and simmer for 30 minutes.

2 Whisk the rest of the ingredients together in a bowl. Drain the ribs, allow to steam for a few minutes to dry off, then place in a roasting tin. Pour the marinade over to coat the ribs well, reserving around 6 tbsp for finishing. Cover with foil and cook in the oven for 1½ hours. The meat should be very tender.

3 Preheat the barbecue or a chargrill pan. Brush most of the reserved marinade over the ribs and cook for a few minutes to create a lovely charred effect. Finish with a final brush of the marinade before serving.

"To split the workload for a large barbecue, complete to the end of Step 1 the day before. Cool quickly, then cover and chill until ready to use." **Jon's tip**

Thyme-roasted pork with pan-fried pears & Perry gravy

We have a saying, here at the cookery school, that what grows together goes together. What better illustration than succulent pork made with juicy ripe pears and a Perry gravy that's good enough to drink on its own, with the health-giving benefits of whole roasted shallots and garlic.

Serves 6 (with leftovers)

2kg leg or belly of pork, boned, rolled and scored
1 tsp sea salt
8 fresh thyme sprigs

For the roasted garlic and shallots:
400-500g shallots (about 18-24)
12 garlic cloves

For the pears:
25g unsalted butter
3 pears, peeled, cored and cut into quarters lengthways
1 tbsp demerara sugar

For the gravy:
500ml Perry (pear cider)
100ml double cream
Freshly ground black pepper

Prepare 45 minutes
Cook 2-2½ hours

Wine suggestion
Try a crisp and refreshing glass of Perry, but it would also suit a New World Chardonnay, or either a Pinot Gris or Pinot Grigio from New Zealand.

1 Remove the pork from the fridge about 30 minutes before cooking. Preheat the oven to 200°C/180°C fan oven/gas mark 6 and dry the pork with clean kitchen paper. Check the skin has been thoroughly scored and, if necessary, add a few more cuts using a sharp knife. Rub the salt well into the skin, then tuck the thyme into the fleshy part of the meat. Tie the joint together with string. Place in a roasting tray.

2 Calculate the cooking time for the pork, allowing 25 minutes per 500g plus 25 minutes. Roast on the highest shelf for the first hour, then turn the oven down to 190°C/170°C fan oven/gas mark 5 for the remaining cooking time.

3 Meanwhile, prepare the roasted shallots and garlic. Put the shallots in a bowl and pour boiling water over the top to cover — this makes it easier to remove the skins. Put the whole garlic cloves in a small saucepan with boiling water, cook for 5 minutes then run them under cold water and peel off the skins.

4 Add the peeled shallots and garlic to the roasting tin about 45 minutes before the end of cooking time. When the pork is cooked and the juices run clear, transfer to a serving plate, cover with foil to keep warm and leave to rest for 15 minutes. Using a slotted spoon, transfer the shallots and garlic to a heatproof serving dish, leaving behind a few garlic cloves to mash into the pan juices. Keep warm until you're ready to serve.

5 While the pork is resting, heat the butter in a frying pan and fry the pear quarters until tender and golden. After a minute or two, stir in the sugar, turning the heat to low if the pears are browning too much but are still not soft. Spoon into a serving dish and keep warm.

6 Place the roasting tray with the pan juices directly on to the hob. Scrape in any residue stuck to the pan and mash in the reserved garlic cloves. Add the Perry, bring to the boil and pour in the cream (don't worry if it looks as though it's curdling). Let the gravy bubble and reduce until it reaches a good sauce consistency. Season with some freshly ground black pepper and pour into a gravy boat to serve with the pork and the pears.

Cornish steak pasty

The Cornish pasty is reckoned to be over 700 years old, but it came into its own in the 17th century as a self-contained, portable lunchbox, edible from end to end. Various versions have surfaced over the centuries, including one clever idea of jam at one end and meat at the other – a main course and pudding in one! This recipe is simple and really tasty.

Serves 6

For the pastry:
150g strong plain flour
300g plain flour, plus extra for
    rolling out
½ tsp salt
50g butter, cubed
225g white vegetable shortening,
    chilled and cut into small pieces

For the filling:
150g swede
250g floury potatoes, peeled
150g onion, chopped
400g chuck steak, cut into 1cm
    pieces
1 tsp salt
¾ tsp freshly ground black pepper

1 medium egg, beaten

Prepare 1 hour, plus 6 hours chilling
Cook 50 minutes

1 To make the pastry, sift the flours and salt into a bowl, then add the butter and rub in with your fingertips until the mixture resembles fine breadcrumbs.

2 Stir in the vegetable shortening, followed by 225ml cold water, then use a round-bladed knife to bring everything together into a soft dough. Knead briefly on a board until smooth, wrap in cling film and chill in the fridge for 4 hours.

3 Unwrap the dough and roll out on a lightly floured surface into a long, thin rectangle about 1cm thick. Fold up the bottom third, then fold down the top third and roll out once more. Repeat this process until all pieces of fat have disappeared. Fold up the dough once more and wrap in cling film and return to the fridge for 1 hour.

4 Prepare the filling by cutting all the vegetables into very small pieces. Cut the swede and potatoes into 1cm thick slices, then slice each one lengthways into 1cm thick chips. Cut these across into 5mm thick pieces. Mix the swede, potatoes, onion and steak together in a bowl with the salt and pepper.

5 On a floured surface or board, roll out the dough to a thickness of 3mm and cut out 6 x 20cm discs. Spoon one-sixth of the filling into the centre of each pastry disc and lightly brush the edge of one half of the disc with cold water.

6 Bring the edges together over the top of the filling and press together well. Working from left to right, fold in the corner and then fold 2½cm of the edge inwards. Continue like this along the edge to create a rope-like design that will form a seam along the pasty. Chill in the fridge for 1 hour.

7 Preheat the oven to 180°C/160°C fan oven/gas mark 4. Transfer the pasties to a greased baking sheet, brush with beaten egg and bake for 50 minutes, turning halfway through cooking to ensure even browning. Serve warm.

Rack of lamb with braised peas, bacon, lettuce & mint

What could be more traditional, simple and nourishing than lamb cooked this way? What's more, it's just as delicious if you substitute a piece of roasted white fish, such as cod or monkfish, and serve it with buttered new potatoes and lightly cooked frozen petits pois or fresh peas when in season. Frozen peas lock in all the vitamin C so you get the full benefit.

Serves 4

30g butter
1 large onion, finely chopped
Salt and freshly ground black pepper
6 rashers smoked, streaky bacon, cut into batons
250g petits pois
2 small baby gem lettuce, finely shredded
1 tbsp vegetable oil
2 large racks of lamb, fully trimmed
4 tbsp Madeira or Marsala
500ml lamb stock
Squeeze lemon juice
Small bunch fresh mint, leaves picked and finely chopped
Small bunch fresh flat-leaf parsley, leaves picked and finely chopped

Prepare 10 minutes
Cook 40-45 minutes

1 Preheat the oven to 200°C/180°C fan oven/gas mark 6. In a large saucepan, melt 25g of the butter and gently fry the onion with a small pinch of salt until softened (set aside the remaining butter to use later). Add the bacon and continue to fry until the bacon and onion are thoroughly cooked, but without browning.

2 Add the peas and lettuce and stir to combine. Cover the saucepan and braise the vegetables for 10 minutes or until tender.

3 Meanwhile, preheat a large ovenproof frying pan over a high heat. When hot, add the oil. Season the lamb, add to the pan and cook for 2-3 minutes on each side to lightly brown, then place the frying pan in the oven and roast for 3 minutes. (If you don't have an ovenproof frying pan, transfer the lamb to a preheated roasting tray and place in the oven.) Remove the lamb from the oven, place on a warm plate, cover with foil and allow to rest.

4 To make the sauce, deglaze the juices in the roasting tin: place it over a medium heat and add the Madeira or Marsala, then let it bubble to reduce until syrupy. Pour in the lamb stock and bring to the boil. Simmer until the sauce has reduced to a light coating consistency. Stir in the remaining butter, the lemon juice and any juices from the roasted lamb. Keep warm.

5 Once the peas and lettuce are cooked, stir through the fresh herbs. Carve each rack of lamb into cutlets and divide equally among four plates with the braised peas and a little of the lamb sauce spooned over.

> **Wine suggestion**
> Wines should match the combination of fragrant flavours, delicious tenderness and moderate intensity, so try an aged Bordeaux from the Médoc, a Rioja, or a Spanish red that has Syrah in the blend. Or for something different, track down a Cabernet Franc.

Lancashire hotpot with pickled red cabbage

This is one of Britain's great regional dishes. Born out of the relative poverty of hardworking families in the north of England in the 19th century, it's tasty and nourishing, yet uses economical cuts of meat along with seasonal ingredients. Red cabbage is a delicious way to get the kids used to eating brassicas, too.

Serves 6

4 lambs' kidneys (optional)
50g butter, melted, for greasing and brushing
1.5kg floury potatoes, such as Maris Piper, peeled and thinly sliced
Salt and freshly ground black pepper
450g onions, halved and thinly sliced
8 best-end lamb chops, bony ends cut off and trimmed of excess fat
2 small-boned lamb shanks or 1 half shoulder, cut into small chunks
2 tsp fresh thyme leaves
500ml lamb stock

For the pickled red cabbage:
450g red cabbage
25g sea salt
300ml balsamic vinegar
2 dried red chillies
2 cloves
1 tsp coriander seeds
1 tsp black peppercorns
Thumb-size piece fresh root ginger, peeled and bruised
½ tsp juniper berries
2 pieces blade mace
2 tsp caster sugar

Prepare 1 hour, plus 4-5 days pickling
Cook 2-3 hours

1 First make the pickled red cabbage 4-5 days before you need it. Discard the outer leaves, cut the cabbage into quarters, then remove and discard the thick white core. Thinly slice the remaining cabbage. Layer it in a large bowl with the salt. Cover with a plate to weight it down and leave in a cool place for 24 hours, stirring occasionally.

2 The following day, rinse the cabbage under cold running water and drain well. Put the vinegar, chillies, cloves, coriander seeds, peppercorns, ginger, juniper berries, mace and sugar into a large pan. Bring to the boil and simmer for 5 minutes, then leave to cool. Pack the cabbage into large sterilised jars, strain over the vinegar and seal. Leave in the fridge for 3-4 days.

3 To make the hotpot, preheat the oven to 170°C/150°C fan oven/gas mark 3. Cut the lambs' kidneys in half (if using) and use scissors to snip out the cores. Discard. Cut the kidneys into thin slices.

4 Put a layer of potatoes in the bottom of a lightly buttered 4.5 litre lidded casserole dish, scatter over some of the onions, half the chops and chunks of shank, some of the kidney (if using) and a few thyme leaves, seasoning well between each layer. Repeat the layers once more, pour over the stock and finish with a neat layer of overlapping potato slices.

5 Brush the top of the potatoes with some of the melted butter, cover the casserole with a tightly fitting lid and cook in the oven for 2 hours.

6 Remove the hotpot from the oven and increase the temperature to 220°C/200°C fan oven/gas mark 7. Take off the lid, brush the potatoes with the remaining melted butter and return to the oven for 30 minutes or until the potatoes are crisp and golden. Bring the dish to the table, with the pickled red cabbage, and let people help themselves.

Slow-cooked beef rendang with cucumber salad

This dish originated in Indonesia, but it's also widely eaten in Malaysia and is a particular favourite with the Muslim community during Eid. The complex flavours develop beautifully if you keep it for a day or two after cooking. Substituting half-fat crème fraîche for the coconut cream in the cucumber salad will cut down on your saturated fat intake.

Serves 4

For the curry:
1 tsp coriander seeds
1 tsp cumin seeds
4cm piece cinnamon stick
6 cloves
4 dried Kashmiri chillies, stalks
   removed
6cm piece fresh root ginger or
   galangal, roughly chopped
4 garlic cloves, finely chopped
1 medium onion, roughly chopped
½ tsp turmeric
500g blade, skirt or chuck beef
   steak, cut into 4cm pieces
2 tbsp tamarind paste
400ml coconut milk
1 tbsp light soft brown sugar
Salt

For the cucumber salad:
½ cucumber, peeled, deseeded and
   sliced
4 tbsp coconut cream
1 large hot red chilli, halved,
   deseeded and thinly sliced
1 medium green chilli, halved,
   deseeded and thinly sliced
1 small red onion, thinly sliced
Juice of 2 limes
Small bunch fresh coriander,
   roughly chopped

Prepare 40 minutes
Cook 2 hours

1 Make the curry paste. Place the coriander and cumin seeds, cinnamon, cloves and dried chillies in a spice grinder and grind to a fine powder. Put the ginger or galangal, garlic, onion and turmeric in a food processor. Add the ground spices and 40ml cold water and blend to a smooth paste.

2 Tip the curry paste into a large, heavy-based pan and add the diced beef, tamarind paste, coconut milk, sugar and 1 tsp salt.

3 Bring to the boil, then turn down to a simmer. Cook, covered, for about 2 hours, stirring occasionally, then stirring more frequently towards the end of cooking as the sauce becomes concentrated. You can add a little water if the sauce is looking too thick or oily.

4 To make the cucumber salad, mix the cucumber and ½ tsp salt together in a bowl and set aside for 3 minutes to draw out the liquid from the cucumber. Pour off the excess liquid and pat the cucumber dry with some kitchen paper. Mix the cucumber with the rest of the salad ingredients, stir everything together well, then serve alongside the beef rendang.

"Don't be tempted to cook this curry too quickly – simmer very gently to achieve a succulent end result."

James B's tip

Chicken 8

Asian pesto chicken with noodles

This is one of our favourites at the cookery school, so easy to make that when we first cooked and ate it, we were just blown away by the simplicity of its flavours. It also works beautifully with cod, haddock, monkfish or any other firm white fish – just decrease the cooking time by a few minutes.

Serves 4

4 skinless, boneless chicken breast
  fillets, around 500g
Olive oil, for brushing
Salt and freshly ground black pepper
275g dried egg noodles

For the pesto:
Small bunch fresh basil, stalks
  included
Large bunch fresh coriander, stalks
  included
50g dry roasted peanuts
2 red chillies, halved, deseeded and
  roughly chopped
1 thumb-sized piece fresh root
  ginger, peeled and chopped or
  grated
1 lemongrass stalk, finely chopped
Grated zest and juice of 1 lime
¼ tsp salt
6 tbsp groundnut oil
1 tsp toasted sesame oil

Prepare 15 minutes
Cook 15 minutes

1 First make the pesto: place all the ingredients except the oils in a food processor and blend to a paste. With the processor running, slowly drizzle in the groundnut and sesame oils, then scrape the mixture into a bowl.

2 Put the chicken on a board. Take a sharp knife and slice through the middle of each breast giving you two thin pieces. Brush each with olive oil and season with salt and pepper. Heat a griddle pan or heavy-based frying pan over a moderate heat. Cook the chicken in two batches, taking care not to overload the pan, for 6-7 minutes each side or until cooked through (the juices should run clear when pierced with a skewer).

3 Meanwhile, cook the noodles according to the packet instructions. Drain thoroughly, then tip back into the pan and toss with most of the pesto. Divide among four plates, then top with the chicken and serve immediately, with extra pesto alongside.

"Try different types of noodles such as rice, egg or udon – each gives its own distinctive texture and flavour to the dish."

Wilson's tip

Poached chicken with wild mushroom & champagne sauce

Simple, easy, delicious! This recipe is from our Simple Suppers course and has proved a great hit. One of our course attendees subsequently added a touch of saffron to the sauce, which gave it another dimension, so that's worth a try. Match it with baby boiled potatoes.

Serves 4

4 chicken breasts
300ml champagne or sparkling dry white wine, such as Cava
300ml chicken stock
1 tsp olive oil
250g wild mushrooms or flat portobellos, halved and thinly sliced
2 tbsp half-fat crème fraîche
1 tbsp freshly chopped tarragon
Salt and freshly ground black pepper

Prepare 10 minutes
Cook 25-30 mniutes

1 Place the chicken breasts in a single layer in a large saucepan. Pour over the champagne or sparkling wine and chicken stock, cover and bring to the boil. Reduce the heat and simmer gently for 15-20 minutes, until the chicken breasts are thoroughly cooked.

2 Heat the oil in a frying pan and cook the mushrooms for 2-3 minutes, turning occasionally, until golden.

3 Strain the liquor from the chicken into a bowl and set aside the chicken, keeping it warm. Add the reserved liquor to the mushrooms and allow to bubble for 3-4 minutes. Reduce the heat and stir in the crème fraîche and tarragon. Simmer gently for 2-3 minutes, until the sauce has thickened slightly. Season to taste.

4 Slice the chicken breasts diagonally into thick slices and arrange on four warmed serving plates. Pour over the sauce and serve straightaway.

"Try other varieties of mushrooms for a deeper, more complex flavour. Fresh shiitake, chestnut and enoki all work well."

Wilson's tip

Chicken

Yakitori chicken

'Yakitori' means grilled, but these days it's applied to skewered meats of any sort. Keep it simple and eat these as they are enjoyed in Japan - with friends and plenty of ice-cold beer.

Serves 4

4 skinless, boneless chicken thighs, cut into 1.5cm cubes
2 tsp sugar
4 tbsp soy sauce
4 tbsp mirin
2 tbsp sake
1 tbsp sunflower oil, for brushing
Pinch salt

Prepare 10-15 minutes, plus marinating
Cook 8-10 minutes

1 Place the chicken, sugar, soy sauce, mirin and sake in a large bowl. Mix to combine well then place in the fridge for 20 minutes, or overnight if time allows. Soak 12 wooden skewers in a bowl of cold water.

2 Remove the chicken pieces from the marinade (reserve the marinade for later). Thread the chicken on to the soaked wooden skewers.

3 Place the reserved marinade into a small saucepan and reduce over a high heat for about 3-4 minutes until thoroughly cooked and lightly syrupy. Remove from the heat and allow to cool a little.

4 When ready to cook, preheat the barbecue or place a griddle pan over a high heat. Brush the chicken lightly with sunflower oil and place the skewers on the barbecue or in the chargrill pan and cook for 5-6 minutes, turning once or twice. Make sure the chicken is thoroughly cooked through - the juices should run clear when the flesh is pierced with a skewer or a knife.

5 Remove the yakitori skewers from the grill, brush with the reduced marinade and place on a serving plate. Season lightly with salt and serve.

Wine suggestion
Sake's soft fruitiness, served either warm or chilled, would go well here. Rosé d'Anjou would also work well with the sweetness of the marinade.

"Slip some vegetables between each piece of chicken – chunks of red pepper, slices of asparagus or button mushrooms will make this dish even healthier."

Wilson's tip

Southern-style spicy chicken

Traditionally, Southern-style spicy chicken is deep-fried, but this is much healthier, as it's cooked in the oven. However, it still retains every bit of its comforting appeal.

Serves 4

100g fresh white breadcrumbs
2 tbsp thyme, finely chopped
2 tbsp parsley, finely chopped
1 tsp cayenne pepper
2 tsp paprika
Salt and freshly ground black pepper
2 medium eggs
4 chicken drumsticks and 4 chicken
    thighs
4 tbsp plain flour, seasoned
3 tbsp olive oil

Prepare 20 minutes
Cook 25-30 mniutes

1 Preheat the oven to 200°C/180°C fan oven/gas mark 6. In a flat dish, mix together the breadcrumbs, herbs, spices and some seasoning.

2 Put the eggs in a shallow bowl and beat lightly. Coat the chicken portions in the seasoned flour, dip them first into the egg then into the breadcrumb mixture to coat thoroughly. Place on a baking sheet.

3 Drizzle with the oil and cook in the oven for 25-30 minutes, turning once, until the crumb coating is crisp and the chicken is cooked thoroughly, and the juices run clear when pierced with a skewer.

"Make a quick dip to serve with this by mixing together 100ml creme fraiche, 2 tbsp chopped fresh chives, 1 crushed garlic clove. Season with freshly ground black pepper and serve." **Gordon's tip**

Stir-fried Sichuan chicken with cashew nuts & spring onions

This style of Chinese cooking originated in the Sichuan Province of southwestern China, renowned for its bold and pungent flavours, which are still a major feature of its cuisine. This combination of chicken with creamy cashews and fiery chillies is a quick and easy midweek meal that never disappoints.

Serves 4

3 large skinless chicken breasts, diced into 2.5cm pieces
1 medium egg white
6 tsp cornflour
3 tbsp light soy sauce
4 tbsp sunflower oil
85g unsalted, unroasted cashew nuts
Salt
2 large red chillies, halved, deseeded and finely chopped
1 tsp granulated or caster sugar
2 tsp white wine vinegar
6 spring onions, finely sliced

Prepare 30 minutes, plus marinating
Cook 20 minutes

1 Place the chicken in a bowl and mix in the egg white, followed by 4 tsp of the cornflour. Make sure the chicken is well coated then cover and chill in the fridge for a minimum of 10 minutes, or up to 3 hours.

2 Mix the remaining cornflour with the soy sauce and 150ml cold water.

3 When you're ready to serve, heat 1 tbsp of the oil in a wok until hot. Add the cashew nuts and a pinch of salt and stir-fry for a few seconds until golden brown. Transfer to a plate lined with kitchen towel to drain and dry. Set aside.

4 Return the wok to the heat and add the remaining oil. Once hot, add the chillies, marinated chicken and sugar. Stir-fry briskly for about 5 minutes until the chicken is golden and thoroughly cooked, with no pink meat visible. Stir in the vinegar and allow it to evaporate.

5 Add the cornflour and soy sauce mixture with the cashew nuts and spring onions. Add more seasoning, or sugar, if desired.

6 As soon as the sauce has thickened, remove from the heat and serve immediately.

"If you don't fancy chicken breast, try pork fillet diced to the same size – it will take the same length of time to cook." **Gordon's tip**

Clay pot chicken rice

This dish is typical of what you'll find at street stalls in Singapore. Just looking at those little clay cauldrons of amazing oriental flavour on the open fires is enough to make your mouth water. If you add some sweet Chinese sausage, it makes all the difference.

Serves 4

2 skinless, boneless chicken breasts, cut into 2cm cubes
400g jasmine rice, washed
750ml light chicken stock
1 Chinese sausage (lap cheung), sliced (optional)
8 shiitake mushrooms, stalks removed and discarded, sliced
3cm piece fresh root ginger, peeled and minced

For the marinade:
40ml sunflower oil
100ml oyster sauce
40ml light soy sauce
20ml dark soy sauce
20ml Shaoxing rice wine or dry sherry
1 tbsp sesame oil
1 tbsp chilli oil
2 tsp caster sugar
1 tbsp cornflour
½ tsp freshly ground white pepper

To garnish:
2 spring onions, finely sliced
4 tbsp finely chopped fresh coriander

Prepare 15 minutes, plus marinating
Cook 35-45 minutes

1 Preheat the oven to 180°C/160°C fan oven/gas mark 4. Combine all the marinade ingredients in a large bowl and add the chicken. Toss well to mix everything together and ensure the chicken is well coated with the marinade. Cover and place in the fridge for up to 2 hours, or up to 4 hours if you have time.

2 Put the rice in a heavy-based ovenproof saucepan (traditionally, a clay pot would be used), pour over the chicken stock, then cover and cook over a low heat on the hob for 15-20 minutes.

3 Spread the marinated chicken, Chinese sausage, mushrooms and ginger over the top of the rice. Cover and transfer to the oven and continue to cook for 20 minutes until the rice and chicken are cooked through.

4 Remove from the oven, taste and adjust the seasoning if necessary. Scatter over the spring onions and coriander and serve immediately.

"When you're cooking the rice, stir it only once. Over-stirring can make it heavy and sticky."

Wilson's tip

Chicken shawarma

Right across the Middle East, shawarma is the fast food of choice. Basically, it's a flatbread wrap with a juicy filling - not a million miles away from the idea of the British sandwich. Although more commonly made with lamb, we've used chicken, which makes for a healthy and light, yet satisfying, lunch.

Serves 4

2 large onions, roughly chopped
4 tbsp baharat (Arab spice mix)
4 garlic cloves, crushed
Finely grated zest and juice of 1 lemon
2 tbsp extra virgin olive oil
Salt and freshly ground black pepper
8 boneless chicken thigh fillets, skin on
4 Lebanese flatbreads or wraps
2 large tomatoes, very thinly sliced
1 red onion, very thinly sliced

For the garlic sauce:
4 garlic cloves, left whole, papery skins intact
4 tbsp extra virgin olive oil
Juice of 1 lemon

Prepare 30 minutes, plus marinating
Cook 15 minutes

1 To make the marinade, place the onions in a food processor and process in bursts until very finely chopped. Tip the chopped onions on to a piece of muslin, pull the corners together and squeeze to extract the onion juice into a large bowl. Whisk in the baharat, garlic, lemon zest and juice and olive oil. Season well with salt and pepper then add the chicken, rubbing the marinade in well. Cover and place in the fridge to marinate for 15-20 minutes, or preferably overnight.

2 For the garlic sauce, place the garlic in a small saucepan, cover with cold water, bring to the boil and cook over a high heat for 30 seconds. Remove the garlic and peel. Place in a mortar bowl with a good pinch of salt and, using a pestle, pound for 2-3 minutes until very smooth. Gradually add the olive oil, then the lemon juice in a thin stream, while pounding and mixing well (if the mixture looks like it will split, add a tablespoon of hot water).

3 Preheat a chargrill pan over a high heat. Remove the chicken from the marinade and dry well with clean, dry kitchen paper. Place the chicken skin side down in the pan and cook for 8-10 minutes, turning occasionally, until lightly charred and firm to the touch. Make sure the chicken is thoroughly cooked with no pink meat - the juices should run clear when pierced with a skewer.

4 Remove the chicken, place on a chopping board and allow to rest for 2-3 minutes, then carve into finger-sized pieces.

5 To serve, place each flatbread on a plate, spread with the garlic sauce, top with tomato, onion and chicken, and roll up.

"This recipe works really well on a charcoal barbecue. Make sure you begin with the chicken skin side down — this helps break down the fat and crisps the skin." **Claire's tip**

Moroccan chicken with preserved lemons & olives

Preserved lemons are usually pickled in salt and their own juice. They're a favourite ingredient in Moroccan tagines and sauces, and give them their unique flavour.

Serves 4

1.5kg whole free-range chicken
1 large onion, finely chopped
4 garlic cloves, crushed
100g unsalted butter
1½ tbsp ground ginger
2 cinnamon sticks
¾ tsp turmeric
¾ tsp saffron strands
Salt and freshly ground black pepper
3 tbsp lemon juice
100g Kalamata olives
4 small preserved lemons, halved
50g chicken livers, chopped
Small bunch coriander, roughly
    chopped
2 tbsp flat-leaf parsley, roughly
    chopped

Prepare 30 minutes
Cook 2 hours

1 Place the chicken in a tagine, if you have one, or else a flameproof casserole or saucepan with a well-fitting lid - it needs to fit snugly to ensure quick and even cooking. Add the onion, garlic, butter, ginger, cinnamon sticks, turmeric, saffron and some seasoning. Pour in 700ml cold water, cover and bring to the boil over a medium to high heat. Reduce the heat and leave to simmer, spooning the sauce over the chicken and turning it occasionally until just cooked through – about 40 minutes. Lift the chicken on to a plate and cover with foil.

2 Add the lemon juice to the casserole, increase the heat and simmer the sauce rapidly, uncovered, until reduced by about two-thirds. Return the chicken to the casserole with the olives and preserved lemons. Cover with a well-fitting lid and simmer for a further 20-25 minutes until the chicken is tender and there is no pink meat visible. Lift the chicken on to a large, pre-warmed platter and cover again with foil.

3 Add the chicken livers to the sauce and simmer for 5 minutes. Sprinkle in the herbs and adjust the seasoning if necessary. Spoon the sauce over the chicken and serve with couscous (see tip below).

> **Wine suggestion**
> Montepulciano d'Abruzzo or Chianti, with their bright red berry fruit flavours, will complement the herbs and spices.

"Couscous is a delicious side dish here — mix parsley, chives and a good squeeze of lemon with couscous prepared according to the packet instructions."

Jon's tip

Summer chicken with new potatoes, peas & mint

This is one of our simplest chicken recipes - easy ingredients that are quick to put together, with zingy mint to give the dish its summery character. Perfect for laid-back living.

Serves 4

2 tbsp olive oil
4 chicken breasts, skin on
2 shallots, finely sliced
1 garlic clove, crushed
20 small new potatoes, scrubbed
    and quartered
200ml chicken stock
Salt and freshly ground black pepper
190g fresh peas or frozen petits pois
2 tbsp crème fraîche
2 tbsp fresh mint, chopped

Prepare 10 minutes
Cook 25 minutes

1 Heat the oil in a large, deep frying pan and add the chicken breasts, skin side down. Cook for 3 minutes until the skin has taken on some colour, then turn and cook for a further 3 minutes. Add the shallots, garlic and potatoes and cook, stirring occasionally, for 3-4 minutes.

2 Pour in the chicken stock and season. Bring to the boil, then cover and simmer gently for about 10 minutes.

3 Add the peas and simmer for a further 3-4 minutes, or until the peas are tender and the chicken and potato are thoroughly cooked. Stir in the crème fraîche and mint and simmer again for a minute or two until the sauce has thickened slightly. Serve immediately.

Wine suggestion
This is a wonderfully versatile dish for wine - it can take a light red, bright white or even a rosé with ease. Try a New World Pinot Noir, a white Burgundy (from the Mâcon or Côte Chalonnaise) or a Southern French rosé.

"Leftover chicken makes a tasty salad: shred it and add baby spinach, cherry tomatoes and thinly sliced cucumber. Toss with a dash of white wine vinegar and extra virgin olive oil."

Wilson's tip

Chicken katsu curry

Somehow, curry is not what we immediately associate with the Japanese kitchen, and yet it's very common there. It was introduced to the country in 1872, with the first Japanese curry powder appearing in shops in 1923, after which it took off like a rocket and became a household staple. Although we use chicken in this recipe, pork fillet is a good substitute.

Serves 4

For the chicken:
4 medium eggs
40g plain white flour
200g dried Panko breadcrumbs
260g skinless, boneless chicken thighs
Vegetable oil, for frying
Salt

For the curry sauce:
40g unsalted butter
½ large onion, finely chopped
2 garlic cloves, chopped
100g apple, peeled and finely chopped
2 tsp curry powder
½ tsp turmeric
600ml chicken stock
200ml coconut milk
2 tbsp honey
60g sugar snap peas, blanched and halved

Prepare 10 minutes
Cook 25 minutes

1 Mix the eggs together in a bowl and set aside. Place the flour in a second bowl, then pour the Panko breadcrumbs into a third bowl. Coat the chicken by first dipping it in the flour, then in the egg and finally in the breadcrumbs. Set aside.

2 To make the curry sauce, melt the butter in a frying pan. Add the onion and fry over a gentle heat until soft and golden. Add the garlic and apple and cook for a further 3 minutes.

3 Add the curry powder and the turmeric and stir through, then add the stock, coconut milk, honey and sugar snap peas. Bring to the boil and simmer for 8 minutes. Add a pinch of salt to taste and set aside.

4 Heat the vegetable oil in a heavy-based pan. Check the heat by dropping some breadcrumbs in - when they sizzle it's ready for cooking. Add the chicken to the pan and fry over a medium heat for 8 minutes, turning over halfway through. Check the chicken is cooked by slicing each piece in half and making sure there are no pink juices. Place on a piece of kitchen towel and season with a little salt.

5 Serve with the warm curry sauce.

Puddings 9

Baked yoghurt with stewed fruit

This recipe is dead easy, but not everyone knows that, so you'll look great serving it to your friends. We're using strawberries here, which are perfect in summer; but in winter we do it with poached rhubarb - the tartness cuts nicely through the richness, balancing it perfectly.

Serves 4

For the baked yoghurt:
200g condensed milk
250g natural yoghurt
200g whipping cream

For the strawberry compote:
200g strawberries, hulled, washed
    and chopped
20g icing sugar
Greek basil, to serve

Prepare 30 minutes
Cook 30 minutes

1 Preheat the oven to 150°C/130°C fan oven/gas mark 2.

2 Put the condensed milk in a bowl and add the yoghurt and whipping cream. Whisk together until smooth, pour into four 200ml ramekins (or ovenproof glasses), then place them in a roasting tin. Pour about 3mm hot water into the bottom of the tin and bake for 20 minutes. Remove the tin from the oven, immediately lift the ramekins out and allow to cool, then transfer to the fridge to chill.

3 Put the strawberries in a bowl, add the icing sugar and mix together. Set aside to macerate for at least 30 minutes and then chill until you're ready to serve.

4 To assemble the dish, divide the strawberries among the four ramekins and spoon the juices over the top. Garnish with the basil leaves and serve.

"When you're pouring the water into the bottom of the roasting tin to cook the ramekins, make sure the water is hot right from the beginning — this will speed up the cooking process."

James C's tip

216

Whisky nut tarts with Baileys Irish Cream

These tarts are utterly delicious - adding whisky gives an acerbic kick to an otherwise unrelieved sweetness, balancing the flavours.

Serves 4

For the tarts:

200g sweet pastry (see pages 32-33)
Plain flour, for rolling out
Vegetable oil, for greasing
100g unsalted butter
100g soft dark brown sugar
20g golden syrup
2 medium eggs
Zest of 1 lemon
60g currants
100g sultanas
2 tbsp whisky
50g pecan nuts, roughly chopped

For the Baileys Irish Cream:

150g mascarpone
1 tbsp Baileys Irish Cream liqueur

Prepare 40 minutes, plus 1 hour resting and cooling
Cook 45-50 minutes

1 Preheat the oven to 180°C/160°C fan oven/gas mark 4. Roll the pastry out on a lightly floured board to around 2mm thick and cut out four x 12cm circles. Lightly grease four x 8cm tart tins and line with the pastry, allowing a slight overhang. Transfer to the fridge to rest for about 10 minutes.

2 To make the Baileys Irish Cream, whisk the mascarpone and Baileys together in a bowl. Refrigerate for at least 1 hour.

3 Line the tart cases with baking parchment and baking beans. Cook in the oven for around 15-20 minutes, until golden. Remove the parchment and beans, then carefully trim off the excess pastry around the top. Reduce the oven temperature to 160°C/140°C fan oven/gas mark 2-3.

4 To make the filling, put the butter, sugar and golden syrup into a pan and heat gently, stirring until the sugar dissolves. Remove from the heat and allow to cool slightly. Whisk in the eggs one at a time until combined.

5 In a large bowl, combine the lemon zest, currants, sultanas and whisky, then add the melted butter mixture, stirring well. Add the pecans and fold them into the mixture, then divide the mix equally among the tart cases. Return to the oven and bake for around 12-15 minutes or until just set in the middle. Remove and allow to cool slightly.

6 Remove the tarts from the tins and serve warm with a dollop of the cream.

Apple tarte tatin with clotted cream

When you make this sumptuous pud, take the caramel to the point where it's just starting to smoke before you add the butter. It will have developed a slight bitterness, which balances the richness beautifully.

Serves 4-6

40g liquid glucose
200g caster sugar
90g unsalted butter, diced
1 x 500g packet puff pastry
2 pink lady apples
Plain flour, for rolling out
250g clotted cream, to serve

Prepare 20 minutes
Cook 40 minutes

Wine suggestion

Try a sweet Vouvray (made from Chenin Blanc in the Loire) or a cool-climate late harvest Muscat (from the Limarí Valley in Chile). These will match the combination of this dessert's sweetness and fresh fruit.

1 Preheat the oven to 200°C/180°C fan oven/gas mark 6.

2 Put the glucose into a heavy-based pan, place over a medium heat and warm for 1-2 minutes. Gradually add the sugar and cook, stirring occasionally, until the mixture turns a rich caramel colour. (Don't add all the sugar at once, as it will form lumps and cause the sugar to crystallise.)

3 Take the pan off the heat and gradually stir in the butter. The mixture will bubble up at this stage, so be careful when stirring. Pour the caramel into a traditional tarte tatin mould or an ovenproof frying pan.

4 Roll out the puff pastry on a lightly floured, clean work surface to about 2mm thick. Prick all over with a fork, then cut out a round to the same size as the top of the tatin mould or frying pan. Place on a baking sheet lined with baking parchment and freeze while you complete Step 5.

5 Peel and core the apples, then cut each into 4 wedges. Arrange the apples on top of the caramel, put the puff pastry round on top and bake for 40 minutes. Allow to cool slightly, then turn out carefully on to a serving plate, drizzling any extra sauce around the tart.

6 Cut into pieces and serve with clotted cream.

Steamed marmalade pudding with seared oranges & vanilla custard

This is an old family favourite from the great canon of British steamed puddings - a classic recipe with a modern twist. We've dried and charred the oranges to give it a seductive, smoky flavour.

Serves 6

2 oranges
50g unsalted butter, softened, for
    greasing the moulds
50g plain flour, for dusting the
    moulds
140g marmalade
200g unsalted butter
200g caster sugar
4 medium eggs
400g plain flour
10g baking powder
60ml milk approx.

For the compote:
100g caster sugar
25ml orange juice (leftover juice
    from segments, or store-bought)
20ml Grand Marnier

Prepare 35 minutes
Cook 30 minutes, plus 2 hours
    drying

Wine suggestion
Grab the chance to drink a truly indulgent wine here - Tokaji, with its opulent flavours of marmalade and caramel. Look out for the number of 'Puttonyos' on the label - the higher the number, the sweeter the wine. Number 5 is ideal.

1 Zest the oranges and set aside - this goes into flavouring the pudding later. Peel the oranges using a sharp knife to remove all the pith, then cut out each segment. Place the segments on a baking sheet and leave to dry out for 2 hours at room temperature. Blow torch them or grill them lightly until they have a slightly scorched tinge to them. Set aside for the compote.

2 Take six x 175ml pudding moulds and brush with the softened butter. Add the flour to one mould and tip it around until the buttered surface is completely coated in flour, then transfer the remaining flour to the next mould, and so on until all are coated. Divide the marmalade equally between the moulds and set aside.

3 In a bowl, cream together the butter and the sugar until pale and fluffy, then slowly beat in the eggs. Sieve together the flour and the baking powder and fold into the mixture with the reserved orange zest. Finally, add the milk to soften the texture - you're looking for a good 'dropping' consistency where the mixture drops off the spoon easily in one lump. Spoon the mixture among the six moulds - it should come roughly three-quarters of the way up the sides.

4 Transfer the puddings on to a steamer petal inside a pan containing a couple of centimetres of boiling water. (An upturned plate will work, too.) Cover the pan with a lid and steam for 30 minutes, checking the water level halfway through to make sure it doesn't run dry. The puddings will be ready when they are pierced with a knife or skewer and it comes out clean.

5 For the compote, place a medium pan over a medium heat and gradually add the sugar. It will start to dissolve and slowly turn golden as the heat cooks it. You may need to shake the pan every now and then so that the sugar cooks evenly. When caramelised and a dark golden colour, remove from the heat and, whisking all the time, very carefully add the orange juice and Grand Marnier. Once it is all incorporated, add the reserved orange segments for decorating.

6 Run a knife round the edge of the puddings and upturn each on to a separate plate. Shake the tin a little if it feels like it's sticking. Place 3 or 4 orange segments on top and spoon over the syrup. Serve with crème anglaise (see pages 38-39) or a drizzle of double cream.

Rhubarb Pavlova with lemon yoghurt sorbet

Rather improbably, for a Russian-sounding name, Pavlova was invented by the Kiwis. As soon as you add lemon to a pudding, the tartness sets to work, balancing the sugars. This old favourite just keeps on giving pleasure, generation after generation.

Serves 4

For the sorbet:
150g caster sugar
250g set natural yoghurt
1½ lemons, zest of 1 and juice of all

For the Pavlova:
4 medium egg whites
140g caster sugar
140g icing sugar, sieved

For the rhubarb compote:
400g rhubarb
50g caster sugar

For the lemon vanilla syrup:
Juice of 2 medium lemons
100g caster sugar
Seeds from 1 vanilla pod

To garnish:
Few sprigs Greek basil

Prepare 1 hour
Cook 35 minutes, plus 24 hours
   infusing

1 For the sorbet, first make the sugar syrup: boil 150ml water and the sugar together to make a sugar syrup. Set aside to cool. Whisk the remaining ingredients together with 250ml sugar syrup, then chill and allow to infuse for 24 hours. Spoon the sorbet into a freezer-proof container and freeze while you make the Pavlova.

2 To make the Pavlova, preheat the oven to 100°C/90°C fan oven/gas mark ¼, then whisk the egg whites using an electric beater. Once the egg whites have doubled in volume, gradually add the caster sugar. Whisk on full speed for about 10 minutes - the resulting meringue mixture will seem overwhisked, but that's perfect for this recipe. Gently fold in the icing sugar in three stages. Transfer to a piping bag and pipe on to baking parchment in four equal portion sizes. (If you'd rather a more home-styled look, you can just spoon the mixture on to the parchment instead.) Transfer to the oven and bake for between 1 hour and 1 hour 20 minutes. When cooked, the meringues should lift off the tray leaving no residue underneath. Set aside to cool.

3 To make the rhubarb compote, wash the rhubarb if required, then chop it roughly. Place in a saucepan and add the caster sugar. Cover the pan and transfer to the heat. As the rhubarb boils, give the pan a shake and allow to boil fiercely for about 2-3 minutes. Remove from the heat and leave for around 5 minutes, then carefully remove the lid, as there will be a lot of steam. Transfer to a separate container and leave to cool.

4 To make the lemon vanilla syrup, put all the ingredients into a saucepan and place over a medium heat until reduced to a syrupy consistency.

5 To assemble the dish, put each Pavlova on a plate, top with a spoonful of compote and dot small blobs around the plate for decoration. Drizzle over a little juice, then add a large ball of sorbet. Finish with a little lemon vanilla syrup and add a sprinkling of basil leaves.

"Turn any leftover ingredients into an Eton mess by crushing the meringue and arranging it in a glass with the compote and leftover sorbet – add a little whipped cream if you like."

James C's tip

Crêpes suzettes

We owe this dish to 14-year-old assistant waiter Henri Carpentier's faux pas at the Maitre Café de Paris, Monte Carlo, in 1895. As he was preparing a dessert for the Prince of Wales (the future King Edward VII of England) in full public view, it burst into flames. Thinking his career was over before it had begun, he gave it a last quick taste...and never looked back. It takes its name from a lady who was dining with the prince that evening.

Serves 4
(depending on size of frying pan)

For the crêpes:
30g unsalted butter
100g plain flour
25g caster sugar
2 medium eggs
2 medium yolks
200ml milk
1 tbsp vegetable oil

For the suzette sauce:
3 oranges
250ml orange juice
Juice of 2 lemons
180g demerara sugar
2 tsp cornflour

Grand Marnier, to taste

Prepare 30 minutes
Cook 15 minutes

1 To make the batter for the crêpes, melt the butter in a pan until it starts to foam, then continue to cook until it turns brown and gives off a nutty aroma, to make a '*beurre noisette*'.

2 In a large bowl, mix together the flour and sugar, make a well in the centre and, using a whisk, slowly add the eggs plus the egg yolks. Slowly whisk in the milk and then stir in the *beurre noisette*.

3 Pass the mixture through a sieve into a bowl and set aside.

4 To make the suzette sauce, zest 2 of the oranges, and peel and segment all 3, then set aside. Keep any juice and add it to the 250ml orange juice, zest, lemon juice and sugar, then pour the whole lot into a pan. Bring to the boil and simmer until the liquid is reduced by about half.

5 Add the cornflour and continue to whisk while boiling until the mixture starts to thicken. Strain through a sieve into a bowl, add the segmented oranges and keep warm.

6 Put a small dot of vegetable oil in an omelette-sized frying pan and wipe round with a piece of kitchen paper. Heat the pan until hot.

7 Spoon a ladleful of the crêpe batter into the frying pan. Swirl it around so that it covers the base. Cook for a couple of minutes and, as soon as it's set on top and golden underneath, flip it over and cook the other side for 10 seconds. Continue making crêpes until you've got 4 good ones.

8 Fold the 4 crêpes into quarters, put into the pan with the suzette sauce and orange segments. Warm over a medium heat, then add a splash of Grand Marnier and set alight. Serve either in the pan at the table or spoon the crêpes on to plates together with the oranges and the sauce drizzled over.

"You'll probably find you'll have to throw away the first crepe, but subsequent ones will be perfect once you've got the heat right." **Eleni's tip**

Lemon posset with blueberry compote & lemon madeleines

Posset can be traced back to Tudor times, when it was made with eggs, milk and ale – an early version of custard. Madeleines are young French whippersnappers by comparison – they go back only to the 18th century. With this blueberry compote, it's food from the gods.

Serves 4

For the lemon posset:
Zest and juice of 2 lemons
345ml double cream
100g caster sugar

For the blueberry compote:
Zest of ½ lemon, plus 1 tbsp juice
2 tsp icing sugar
100g blueberries
20ml crème de cassis (blackcurrant liqueur)

For the lemon madeleines:
(You'll need a 12-hole mini madeleine mould)
½ vanilla pod, halved
1 tbsp milk
40g unsalted butter, plus extra melted for
    brushing
Zest and juice of 1 lemon
1 large egg
60g caster sugar
75g plain flour
½ tsp baking powder

Prepare 30 minutes, plus 45 minutes chilling
Cook 5-8 minutes

1 To make the lemon posset, put the lemon zest and juice into a medium saucepan and bring to the boil. Set aside.

2 Put the cream and sugar in a saucepan and bring to the boil. Remove from the heat and mix in the lemon mixture that you've just made, then pass it through a fine sieve into a jug. Divide the posset equally between four decorative glasses and refrigerate for 45 minutes or until set.

3 To make the blueberry compote, put all the ingredients into a small pan and heat gently. Transfer to a bowl, cool, then place in the fridge.

4 To make the madeleines, scrape the seeds from the vanilla pod using the tip of a round-bladed knife and place in a saucepan. Drop in the vanilla pod, too, then add the milk, butter and lemon zest and juice. Heat gently to melt the butter - don't allow the mixture to boil.

5 Whisk the egg and sugar in a bowl. In a separate bowl, combine the flour and baking powder. Add the egg mixture to the flour and whisk.

6 Pass the melted butter mixture through a sieve, and gradually beat into the egg mixture. Cover then chill for at least 30 minutes.

7 Preheat the oven to 180°C/160°C fan oven/gas mark 4. Grease the madeleine mould with butter and spoon the mixture into each hole to three-quarters full. Bake for 5-8 minutes until the tops spring back when touched. Use a palette knife to carefully remove them from the mould.

8 To assemble the dessert, spoon some blueberry compote over the top of each lemon posset, place a couple of madeleines on top and serve.

"The recipe for the madeleines makes 20 small cakes – store leftovers in an airtight container for up to 3 days or freeze, wrapped in cling film, for up to a month."

James C's tip

Bakewell tart

Legend has it that, in 1820, the landlady of the White Horse Inn (now called the Rutland Arms) instructed her cook to make a jam tart. Instead of stirring the eggs and almond paste mixture into the pastry, the hapless cook spread it on top of the jam. Her reputation was saved by the fact that it was so sensational we're still making it today.

Serves 14

For the sweet pastry:
135g unsalted butter, at room temperature
90g caster sugar
2 medium eggs, at room temperature
270g plain flour, plus extra for rolling out
2 medium egg yolks, for glazing

For the frangipane filling:
1 x 460g jar raspberry jam
250g unsalted butter
250g caster sugar
5 medium eggs
60g plain flour
190g ground almonds
Zest of 2 lemons

For the icing:
400g fondant icing sugar
2 tsp Grand Marnier
50g flaked almonds, toasted

Prepare 50 minutes
Cook 1 hour 30 minutes, plus 1 hour 40 minutes resting

1 To make the pastry, using a hand-held mixer, cream together the butter and sugar in a bowl until white and fluffy. This can take up to 5 minutes.

2 Gradually beat in the eggs. Once mixed, add the flour. Don't overwork the mixture, or the pastry will shrink too much when cooked. Bring it together with your hands and shape into a disc. Wrap in cling film and chill for 30 minutes minimum.

3 Preheat the oven to 200°C/180°C fan oven/gas mark 6.

4 Remove the pastry from the fridge, unwrap it and, on a clean work surface lightly dusted with flour, roll out to 2mm thick.

5 Line a 26cm deep tart tin, leaving about 1cm of pastry hanging over the edge. Cut off any excess, put the bits together, wrap in cling film, chill and keep for repairing any cracks. Allow to rest for at least 10 minutes in the fridge (this stops the pastry shrinking when it's baked). Bake blind by lining the tin with a piece of baking parchment filled with beans or rice for 30 minutes until the edges turn golden brown. Remove from the oven, take off the parchment, beans or rice, and turn off the oven.

6 Importantly, repair any cracks in the base of the tart by pushing a little leftover pastry down over fine lines. Glaze with the egg yolks and return to the oven (now switched off) for 2 minutes longer. Allow the pastry to cool. Put the tart, still in its case, on a board and use a Microplane grater to saw away the edge of the overhanging cooked pastry.

7 Spread the jam evenly over the base of the tart case and put in the freezer for 30 minutes to ensure that the jam sets and doesn't bubble up during cooking.

8 To make the frangipane filling, cream the butter and sugar in a bowl until light and fluffy. Add the eggs gradually, beating all the time to prevent curdling.

9 Fold in the flour, ground almonds and lemon zest, then chill for 1 hour.

10 Preheat the oven to 170°C/150°C fan oven/gas mark 3. Spread the frangipane mixture over the jam. Bake for around 35-40 minutes or until golden and cooked all the way through. Check this by inserting a skewer into the middle - it should come out clean. Remove from the oven and cool in the tin.

11 To make the icing, whisk the icing sugar, Grand Marnier and 2 tbsp water together in a bowl (the consistency should look like emulsion paint). Remove the tart from the tin, brush the icing mixture all over, sprinkle with the flaked almonds and chill until set - this will take around 20 minutes. Slice and serve.

"When you're making the pastry, make sure all the ingredients are at room temperature – this helps prevent curdling."

James C's tip

Date & custard tarts

All the elements of this recipe can be made in advance (the date marinade intensifies if it's kept in the fridge for up to two months, or in the freezer for up to six). Make the custard tart mix a day ahead and keep it in the fridge, leaving only the tartlets to be done on the day - even these keep for up to two days in a cool, dry place if they are wrapped in cling film.

Makes 4

For the sweet pastry tartlet cases:
135g unsalted butter, at room
    temperature
90g caster sugar
2 medium eggs, at room
    temperature
270g plain flour, plus extra for
    rolling out
2 medium egg yolks, for glazing

For the date marinade:
125g dates, stoned
25ml orange juice
25ml dark rum
25g caster sugar
Zest of ½ orange
Zest of ½ lemon
1 teabag
½ vanilla pod, split lengthways

For the custard tart mix:
560ml double cream
100g caster sugar
1 vanilla pod
9 medium egg yolks

Prepare 30 minutes
Cook 1 hour 30 minutes

1 Preheat the oven to 170°C/150°C fan oven/gas mark 3. To make the date marinade, put the dates, orange juice and dark rum in an ovenproof dish. Pour the caster sugar into a small pan, add the orange and lemon zest, teabag and vanilla pod with 50ml water. Bring to the boil. Pour over the date mixture, cover with foil and cook for 30 minutes or until the dates are soft. Set aside to cool. Whiz the mixture in a blender until smooth.

2 To make the pastry, cream the butter and sugar in a bowl using a hand-held mixer until white and fluffy. This can take up to 5 minutes. Gradually beat in the eggs, then add the flour. Don't overwork the mixture or the pastry will shrink too much when cooked. Bring it together with your hands and knead lightly, and shape into a disc. Wrap in cling film and chill for at least 30 minutes.

3 Preheat the oven to 200°C/180°C fan oven/gas mark 6. Take the pastry out of the fridge and roll out to 2mm thick on a clean work surface lightly dusted with flour. Line four x 10cm tartlet moulds, leaving 1cm of pastry hanging over the edges. Cut off any excess bits, wrap in cling film and chill - you'll need this to repair any cracks. Chill the tartlets for 10 minutes to stop the pastry shrinking when baked, then bake blind by lining each tin with baking parchment filled with baking beans, rice or flour. Bake for 25-30 minutes, or until the edges are golden brown. Remove the parchment and beans, rice or flour and bake for 5 minutes longer.

4 Be sure to repair any cracks in the base of the tarts by pushing a little leftover pastry down over any fine lines. Glaze the base with the egg yolks and return to the oven for 2 minutes. Cool. With the tarts still in their cases, use a Microplane grater to saw off the edges of the overhanging pastry.

5 Reduce the oven temperature to 130°C/110°C fan oven/gas mark ½. For the custard tart mix, put the cream, half the sugar and the vanilla pod in a medium pan and bring to the boil. Take off the heat and leave to infuse for 5 minutes.

6 Put the egg yolks and the rest of the sugar in a bowl and mix with a spatula. Add the infused cream mix to the egg mixture and stir gently with a spatula to make a custard. Sieve the custard mix over a bowl to extract the vanilla pod.

7 Spread 1 tbsp date purée over the bottom of each tartlet case. Pour in the custard tart mix and bake on a baking sheet for 20-30 minutes. They are ready when they wobble in the centre but are set around the outside. Remove from their cases, lift on to plates and serve while still warm.

"Serve this with Armagnac ice cream. Follow the recipe on page 39 and simply add Armagnac to taste — but not more than 25ml, otherwise it won't set!" **Eleni's tip**

Pomegranate, coconut & mango salad with coconut sorbet

This is the perfect partner for Thai food, invented by James C, one of our chefs. If you haven't got an ice-cream machine, don't worry: follow the sorbet recipe, but put it on a tray to freeze, then run a fork through every 40 minutes or so.

Serves 4

For the coconut sorbet:
400ml can unsweetened coconut milk
250ml whole milk
115g caster sugar

For the shaved coconut:
100g coconut
75g sugar

Lime leaf and lemongrass dressing:
2 sticks lemongrass
5 dried kaffir lime leaves
50g caster sugar
Zest and juice of ½ lime

Pomegranate, mango, coriander and mint salad:
2 mangoes
1 pomegranate
2 tbsp fresh coriander
2 tbsp fresh mint

Prepare 40 minutes, plus 24 hours marinating
Cook 20 minutes

1 To make the sorbet, put all the ingredients into a saucepan, stir together and bring to the boil. Turn off the heat, cool, then churn in an ice-cream machine until firm. Spoon into a freezer-proof container and freeze.

2 Shave the coconut very thinly using a mandolin. Put the sugar and 150ml water in a pan and heat gently to dissolve. Put the coconut in a bowl and pour the hot sugar syrup over. Cover, cool and store overnight. Drain the coconut and place on a baking sheet lined with baking parchment (but keep the leftover syrup in the fridge or freezer to give an ordinary fruit salad an exotic edge on another day). Cook in a low oven (approximately 170°C/150°C fan oven/gas mark 3) until golden brown, stirring occasionally.

3 Slice and crush the lemongrass gently with a rolling pin or the back of a knife, and chop the lime leaves. Put both into a pan with the sugar and 150ml water, add the lime zest and bring to the boil. Take the pan off the heat and allow to infuse for 20 minutes. Pass through a sieve resting on a bowl. Stir the lime juice into the syrup and set aside.

4 Halve the mangoes to remove the stone, then peel each half and dice the flesh. Break the pomegranate in half and separate the seeds (see James C's tip opposite). Chop the herbs.

5 Mix the fruit salad and the syrup dressing in a large serving bowl and add the coconut shavings, reserving a few for decoration. Gently stir through the herbs. Place three or four balls or quenelles of coconut sorbet on top and sprinkle with the reserved coconut. Serve straightaway.

"To separate the membrane from the seeds of the pomegranate, pop them into a bowl of cold water – this should make the membrane float to the top."

James C's tip

Cranachan

This old Scottish summer dish was a harvest-time favourite, when it used to be brought to the table as individual ingredients for people to assemble in the proportions that suited them. Happily, it's an all-year-round treat nowadays.

Serves 4

For the shortbread:
56g plain flour
25g farola or semolina
25g caster sugar
Pinch salt
56g soft butter

For the cranachan:
50g oatmeal
400ml whipping cream
60ml whisky
50g honey
250g raspberries

Prepare 25 minutes
Cook 20 minutes

1 Preheat the oven to 180°C/160°C fan oven/gas mark 4.

2 To make the shortbread: place all the dry ingredients in a bowl and rub the butter into the mix with your fingers until it becomes crumbly. Continue to rub in until it comes together and resembles a pastry dough.

3 Put the dough between two sheets of parchment and roll out to a thickness of around 5mm. Chill for 10 minutes.

4 Remove from the fridge and peel off the top layer of parchment. Put on a baking sheet and bake for 10 minutes.

5 To make the cranachan: sprinkle the oatmeal on to a lipped baking sheet and toast in the oven underneath the shortbread for around 10 minutes or until golden brown. Allow to cool completely.

6 Meanwhile, in a bowl whisk together the cream, whisky and honey until it forms soft peaks. Lightly crush the raspberries, then layer four glasses with some of the cream mixture, raspberries and a sprinkling of oatmeal. Continue until you've used up all the ingredients. Break the shortbread into rough wedges and push a piece into each glass, then serve.

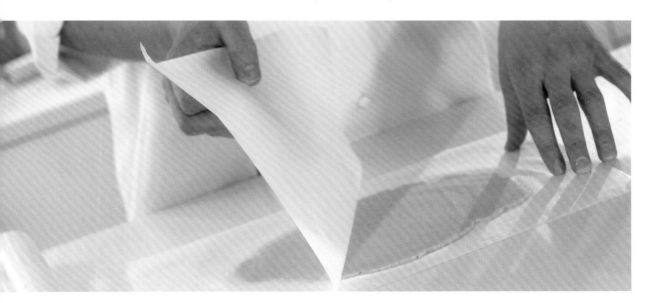

Tiramisù

This translates from the Italian as 'pick me up', thanks to the shot of espresso. It was invented around 1969 by Carminantonio Iannaccone, who had a restaurant in Treviso, north of Venice. He based it on everyday regional flavours - strong coffee, creamy mascarpone, eggs, Marsala and biscuits, and claimed that it took him two years to perfect. Time well spent, we say.

Serves 8

For the zabaglione:
100g egg yolks
60g caster sugar
60ml Marsala

For the mascarpone cream:
375g mascarpone cheese
700ml double cream
125g caster sugar
1 tsp vanilla extract

For the tiramisù:
80ml amaretto
100ml espresso coffee (strong instant will do)
8 Savoiardi biscuits
200g amaretti biscuits, crushed
50-100g cocoa powder, for dusting

Prepare 40 minutes, plus 2 hours chilling

1 Whisk together the egg yolks, caster sugar and Marsala in a heatproof glass bowl using a balloon whisk, then set over a pan of simmering water, making sure the base doesn't touch the water (otherwise known as a '*bain-marie*'). Whisk until the ingredients come together and the mixture leaves a ribbon-like trail.

2 Whip together the mascarpone, double cream, caster sugar and vanilla extract, taking care not to overwhip, or the mixture will become too thick to layer. Set aside and chill for use later.

3 Mix together the amaretto and coffee in a shallow dish. Break each Savoiardi biscuit in half and briefly dip each side into the coffee mixture to soak up a tiny bit of the liquid - you still want texture, not mush. Start to layer up the ingredients in a large serving bowl starting with a layer of biscuits, followed by a spoonful of the zabaglione, followed by mascarpone cream, and repeat the process until the mixture is used up. The idea is that it should look quite homely and rustic. Finally, dust with a little cocoa powder and chill for at least 2 hours before serving.

"You can serve any leftover liqueur as an accompaniment — either drink it or add a touch to your plate if you like."

James C's tip

Churros with chilli hot chocolate sauce

Churros (named after the Churra breed of sheep) is a very old Spanish delicacy originally eaten by shepherds, who had no access to freshly baked produce in the mountains. They adapted a local bread recipe so that they could fry it in a pan over an open fire. No need to chop a chilli for this - it's already in the bar of chocolate.

Serves 4-6

For the churros:

125ml milk
50g unsalted butter
½ tbsp sugar
100g plain flour
Pinch salt
1 large egg
50g caster sugar
Good pinch ground cinnamon
Sunflower or vegetable oil, for deep-
  frying

For the chilli chocolate sauce:

50ml double cream
100g Lindt chilli chocolate (70%),
  chopped

Prepare 10 minutes
Cook 2 minutes

1 To make the churros, bring the milk, butter and sugar to the boil in a small saucepan and keep boiling for 1 minute. Take off the heat and, using a wooden spoon, beat in the flour and salt.

2 Once all the flour is combined, return the saucepan to a low heat. Continue to stir the mixture and cook the flour for 1 minute. It's ready when there's a paste-like film on the base of the pan. Transfer to a bowl and stir for 1 minute to cool.

3 Beat the egg in a bowl and slowly add to the pastry mixture, beating all the time with a wooden spoon to make a choux pastry dough.

4 Place an 8mm star nozzle in a piping bag and transfer the mix into the bag. Mix together the sugar and cinnamon on a plate.

5 Heat a pan of vegetable or sunflower oil - make sure it's hot enough by dipping a teaspoonful of the mix into it. Now, using scissors to cut lengths of 5cm, pipe the rest of the churros mix into the oil. Once they are a golden colour, transfer on to a cooling rack. Coat in the cinnamon sugar while still warm.

6 To make the chilli chocolate sauce, pour the cream into a small pan and bring to the boil. Turn off the heat and add the chocolate. Allow to melt in the heat of the cream, then slowly stir the two ingredients together. Spoon into a bowl and serve with the churros.

Baklava

This delicious honeyed, nutty confection needs little introduction. Its astonishingly long history is said to date back to the wealthy Assyrians of the 8th century BC, who made it with thin layers of bread dough separated by honey and pistachios, believing that they were aphrodisiacs! This recipe has remained pretty much unchanged since the 18th century. Some things stay reassuringly the same.

Makes 24

150g unsalted butter
25 sheets filo pastry
75g whole blanched almonds, chopped finely
75g peeled pistachios, chopped finely
1 tsp ground cinnamon
1 tbsp rose water

For the syrup:
200g caster sugar
1 cinnamon stick
Juice of ½ lemon
1 whole clove

Prepare 30 minutes
Cook 30-40 minutes

1 Preheat the oven to 140°C/120°C fan oven/gas mark 1.

2 First, make the syrup. Put the sugar, 300ml water, the cinnamon stick, lemon juice and whole clove in a pan and bring to the boil. Continue to boil for about 5 minutes, or until the syrup coats the back of a metal spoon. Set aside.

3 Melt 120g of the butter gently in a pan and brush a little over a 40cm x 20cm roasting tin. Cut the filo sheets to fit the size of your roasting tin. Place the first sheet in the roasting tin and, using a pastry brush, spread a thin layer of melted butter over it, then repeat this process until you've brushed 18 sheets, laying one on top of another.

4 Mix the nuts, ground cinnamon and rose water together in a bowl, then spread evenly over the filo.

5 Continue to brush the melted butter over the remaining sheets of filo pastry, laying each sheet on top of the nuts to cover.

6 Cut the baklava into squares (3cm x 3cm), but do not cut right through to the bottom. Melt the remaining 30g butter and use to brush the top layer of filo, and bake for 30-40 minutes.

7 If the top layer hasn't browned, increase the temperature of the oven to 160°C/140°C fan oven/gas mark 2-3 and continue to cook for a further 5 minutes, or until browned. Once you've removed the baklava from the oven, pour the cold syrup over it. Cover with foil and leave in a cool, dry place. This dessert is best served the next day, and can be refrigerated for up to 3 days.

Espresso chocolate mousse with cherry & orange compote

The relationship between chocolate and orange is a time-honoured one, but this version - and presentation - gives it a posh twist. As soon as you top anything with a tuile (French for 'tile') you'll definitely impress anyone who drops by for dinner. For this you'll need a kitchen thermometer - it's cheap and very useful, so well worth having anyway.

Serves 4

For the chocolate mousse:
1 tbsp espresso coffee (or strong instant coffee, if you prefer)
90g caster sugar
4 medium egg yolks
260ml whipping cream
240g dark chocolate (70% cocoa solids), broken into pieces

For the chocolate tuile:
1 tsp cocoa powder
25g icing sugar
2 tsp plain flour
25g demerara sugar
25ml orange juice
30g unsalted butter, melted

For the compote:
1 orange, zested and segmented
50g dried cherries
40g caster sugar

Prepare 50 minutes
Cook 20-25 minutes

1 Preheat the oven to 180°C/160°C fan oven/gas mark 4. Line a baking tray with baking parchment.

2 Start by making the chocolate tuile: sieve together the cocoa powder, icing sugar and flour into a bowl. Add the demerara sugar, orange juice and melted butter, and stir everything together. Set the bowl aside to allow the mixture to rest for 10 minutes. Spread the mixture on to the parchment and bake for 8-10 minutes until dry and matted (if it looks shiny, it's not cooked). Allow to cool, then break into shards.

3 Make the chocolate mousse by mixing the coffee and caster sugar together in a pan, and heating the mixture to 116°C. At the same time, whisk the yolks with an electric whisk until light and fluffy. Pour the hot coffee syrup carefully over the eggs and whisk on half speed until cooled.

4 Meanwhile, whisk the whipping cream in a bowl until thickened and the whisk leaves a ribbon-like trail when removed from the mixture. Melt the chocolate in a bowl over a pan of simmering water making sure the base of the bowl doesn't touch the water. Once the sabayon has cooled, fold in the melted chocolate and the cream. Transfer to a piping bag and pipe (or spoon) into four tumblers. Set aside, but do not refrigerate.

5 To make the compote, place the orange zest in a pan with the cherries and sugar. Bring to the boil and cook for 8-10 minutes until soft. Roughly chop the orange segments, then add to the pan with the cherry mixture. Remove from the heat and cool.

6 To serve, spoon a little compote over each chocolate mousse and decorate with a shard of chocolate tuile.

"Keep any leftover tuiles in an airtight container for up to 2 days — they'll add wow factor to a humble bowl of ice cream."

James C's tip

Hot chocolate with hazelnut cream

This is good to give anyone who doesn't have a wildly sweet tooth – it still feels very rich and indulgent without being cloying.

Makes 10 mugs

For the hot chocolate:
500ml whole milk
225ml whipping cream
75g glucose
30g caster sugar
225g dark chocolate (minimum 70% cocoa solids), chopped

For the hazelnut cream:
150g whipping cream
1 tbsp Frangelico (hazelnut liqueur)

Prepare 10 minutes
Cook 5 minutes

1 Place the milk, cream, glucose and caster sugar in a heavy-based pan and bring to the boil. Whisk in the chocolate and keep warm.

2 To make the hazelnut cream, mix the ingredients together and whip them lightly.

3 Divide the hot chocolate among ten mugs. Spoon the hazelnut cream on to the hot chocolate and serve with the Dark Chocolate & Peppermint Truffles on page 272.

"You can adjust the texture of this drink by adding a little hot water to suit personal preference." **James C's tip**

Baking 10

Carrot cake with cream cheese frosting

Carrot has been used in cakes ever since the Middle Ages simply because it's the second sweetest vegetable there is (sugar beet is the sweetest). This recipe is thought to be Swedish, originally. If you're not big on walnuts, pecan nuts are a good alternative - or use both, if you like.

Serves 12-14

For the cake:
200ml vegetable oil
225g caster sugar
5 medium eggs
1 vanilla pod, split and seeds removed
    or 1 tsp vanilla extract
225g plain flour
1 tsp bicarbonate of soda
1 tsp baking powder
1 tsp salt
1 tsp ground cinnamon
300g grated carrots
200g walnuts, roughly chopped
125g raisins

For the frosting:
350g cream cheese
50g icing sugar
Juice of 1 lemon

Prepare 20 minutes
Cook 1 hour-1 hour 10 minutes

1 Preheat the oven to 170°C/150°C fan oven/gas mark 3, and line a 20cm springform cake tin with baking parchment.

2 Pour the vegetable oil into a large bowl. Add the sugar, eggs, vanilla seeds, flour, bicarbonate of soda, baking powder, salt and cinnamon. Whisk together until smooth. Fold in the grated carrots, 150g of the chopped walnuts and the raisins.

3 Spoon the mixture into the prepared cake tin and bake for 60-70 minutes. Insert a knife or skewer into the centre of the cake to check if it's cooked. If the skewer comes out clean, the cake is ready. If not, cook for a further 5 minutes and check again.

4 Cool in the tin for 5 minutes, then remove and put on to a cooling rack to cool completely.

5 To make the frosting, whisk the cream cheese and icing sugar together in a bowl. When the mixture is light and fluffy, slowly add the lemon juice. Spread the cream cheese frosting on top of the cake using a spoon or a palette knife. Scatter the remaining 50g chopped walnuts over the top to decorate.

Scones

Is there anything more English than a cream tea? It has a special place in our hearts because of its association with lazy summers, jam made from strawberries picked that season, clotted cream and, of course, freshly baked scones. These ones need 4 hours to rest, so start early and set a timer for when they're ready. They're superb, so it's well worth it.

Makes about 10

250g plain flour, plus extra for rolling out
15g baking powder
45g caster sugar, plus a pinch extra
50g butter, diced and chilled
1 medium egg
90ml buttermilk
30g sultanas
1 medium egg yolk, for glazing
Pinch salt
150g clotted cream, to serve

Prepare 10 minutes, plus 4 hours resting (to achieve the perfect finished shape)
Cook 10 minutes

1 Put the flour, baking powder and caster sugar in a large bowl. Add the butter and rub in until the mixture resembles fine breadcrumbs.

2 Stir in the egg and 70ml of the buttermilk (keep the extra 20ml back in case the mixture needs to be softened - it should be sticky, but not stick to your fingers) and mix to make a soft dough, then knead lightly on a board. Divide the dough in two halves, saving one half for plain scones. Fold the sultanas into the other half to make the sultana scones. Wrap each half in cling film and allow to rest at room temperature for 2 hours.

3 Roll out the dough on a lightly floured board to around 3cm thick and cut out rounds with a 5cm plain cutter. Turn the scones over so the flat side is facing up. Beat the egg yolk with the extra pinch of sugar and the salt then brush over the scones to glaze. Do the same again so they have been glazed twice. Put on a baking sheet lined with parchment and rest, uncovered, at room temperature for 2 hours.

4 About half an hour before the scones are ready to bake, preheat the oven to 200°C/180°C fan oven/gas mark 6. Bake for 8-10 minutes until just golden. Serve with jam and a dollop of clotted cream.

Mocha cupcakes with coffee buttercream

This recipe gives a particularly soft texture, simply because the liquid coffee turns the consistency into more of a batter than a cake mix. These are really excellent.

Makes 12

3g instant coffee
175g self-raising flour
225g soft light brown sugar
50g cocoa powder
175g unsalted butter, melted
4 medium eggs, separated

For the coffee buttercream:
100g egg whites
200g caster sugar
300g unsalted butter, chilled and
  diced
30ml coffee
Chocolate-coated coffee beans, to
  decorate

Prepare 1 hour
Cook 15 minutes

1 Preheat the oven to 180°C/160°C fan oven/gas mark 4, and line a 12-hole cake tin with muffin cases.

2 Place the instant coffee in a bowl and dissolve with 90ml boiling water, then set aside to cool.

3 Sift the flour into a bowl and stir in the sugar and cocoa powder. Melt the butter in a medium saucepan, cool a little, then stir in the egg yolks and coffee. Fold into the flour, sugar and cocoa mixture.

4 In a clean, grease-free bowl, whisk the egg whites until soft peaks form, then fold a third into the chocolate mix. Do the same with half of the remaining mixture, and finally fold in the last part.

5 Divide the mixture among the paper cases until each is two-thirds full. Bake for 15 minutes until a skewer inserted into the centre comes out clean.

6 Leave the cupcakes to cool slightly in the tray before turning out on to a wire cooling rack to cool completely.

7 To make an Italian meringue for the coffee buttercream: place the egg whites in an electric mixer fitted with the whisk attachment.

8 Make a sugar syrup by placing the sugar in a pan and adding 100ml water. Heat gently to dissolve the sugar, then stir the edge of the pan with a pastry brush dipped in cold water to wash down any grains of sugar clinging to the side and ensure that no crystals remain. Put a sugar thermometer in the pan and continue to heat the syrup until the temperature reaches 118°C.

9 Whisk the egg whites until soft peaks form. On a medium speed, pour the sugar syrup slowly down the side of the bowl on to the whisked egg whites, taking care that you don't get splashed. When all the syrup has been added, increase to full speed and, after approximately 5 minutes, a white, soft shiny meringue will form.

10 Cool the meringue a little, then add one third of the diced butter and continue to whisk for 3 minutes. Then add the second third and whisk for 3 more minutes before finally adding the remaining third. Once the last portion of butter has been added, the buttercream will have a thick, shiny texture. Whisk in the coffee.

11 Push an 8mm star nozzle into a piping bag and spoon in the coffee buttercream. When the cupcakes are cold, pipe on the buttercream topping and decorate with chocolate-coated coffee beans.

Wholemeal rolls

These rolls have slight sweetness with a crunchy crust and a soft and inviting inside. If you don't have an electric mixer, just make them by hand - we think the process of kneading bread manually is quite therapeutic.

Makes 20

25g dried yeast
600ml lukewarm water
700g plain flour
250g malted grain bread flour
20g salt
60g honey
50g malt extract

Prepare 30 minutes, plus rising and proving
Cook 10-12 minutes

1 Put the yeast in a small bowl and add 100ml of the water. Stir together, then set aside for 10 minutes to allow the yeast to dissolve.

2 Combine the plain flour, malted grain bread flour, salt, honey, malt extract and yeast mixture together in the bowl of an electric mixer.

3 Put a couple of baking trays in a warm oven at 170°C/150°C fan oven/gas mark 3 to heat up. Add the remaining water and knead at a low speed with a dough hook for about 10-15 minutes. When it's ready, divide into 20 even portions and shape into rounds. Sprinkle with flour, place on the preheated trays lined with greaseproof paper and leave to prove in a warm place for 90 minutes until they double in size.

4 Half an hour before the end of the proving process, preheat the oven to 220°C/200°C fan oven/gas mark 7, then bake the rolls for 10-12 minutes.

"Roll the balls on a floured surface or between the palms of both hands. If you're going to score the tops of the rolls, make sure you do it before the proving process, not after."

James C's tip

Zesty palmiers

'Palmier' means 'palm tree' in French, and these biscuits are so called because they're shaped like palm leaves. No one's quite sure where they come from, but they were possibly inspired by the Middle Eastern way of layering pastry with sugar and spices. They first appeared on the saucers of coffee and tea drinkers in Europe sometime in the early 20th century.

Makes about 15

Zest of 1 orange
Zest of 1 lemon
Zest of 1 lime
150g demerara sugar
1 medium egg
2 tsp whole milk
1 x 500g packet puff pastry
Plain flour, for rolling out

Prepare 15 minutes
Cook 8-10 minutes

1 Mix the orange, lemon and lime zest together in a bowl with the demerara sugar. Whisk the egg and milk together in a small bowl. Set both mixtures aside.

2 Roll the puff pastry out on a clean, lightly floured work surface until it's around 3mm thick. Trim the edges to make a square. Put on a lightly floured board then transfer to the freezer for 15-20 minutes to set.

3 Remove the pastry from the freezer and brush both sides with the beaten egg mixture, then sprinkle evenly with the sugar and citrus mixture on both sides. Fold each side of the pastry in from top to bottom so that it meets at the middle, then fold one half on top of the other half and return to the fridge to set again, for 15-20 minutes. Preheat the oven to 190°C/170°C fan oven/gas mark 5.

4 Once the puff pastry strip has set in the fridge, cut into 2cm widths. Place them on a baking tray, lying flat and evenly spaced apart. Bake for 8-10 minutes until golden and crisp all the way through. Cool on a wire rack, then serve.

Millionnaire's shortbread

No one knows why this Scottish confection is called 'millionaire's' shortbread - maybe just because it's so rich, which is quite an achievement considering it's made from such humble ingredients.

Makes 18 pieces

For the base:
150g self-raising flour
90g desiccated coconut
200g golden caster sugar
125g melted butter

For the caramel:
300ml condensed milk
60g butter
2 tbsp golden syrup
125g dark chocolate

Prepare 25 minutes, plus cooling
Cook 20 minutes

1 Preheat the oven to 180°C/160°C fan oven/gas mark 4. Grease and line the base of 30cm x 20cm cake tin with parchment paper.

2 In a large bowl mix together the self-raising flour, desiccated coconut, golden caster sugar and melted butter. It will look crumbly, but don't worry - it comes together once it goes into the tin.

3 Press into the cake tin, level the surface with the back of a metal spoon and bake for 15-20 minutes. The base should be golden and dry to the touch.

4 Meanwhile, put the condensed milk, 30g of the butter and the golden syrup into a saucepan over a medium heat. Once the butter has melted, continue to cook for 5 minutes, whisking continuously. It's ready when the mixture has thickened and is the colour of cloudy honey. (If you don't keep whisking, the caramel will burn and become lumpy.)

5 Spread evenly over the crumble base and return to the oven for a further 10 minutes - the caramel will become a richer golden colour.

6 Melt the chocolate and remaining 30g butter together in a saucepan over a low heat, or in a microwave on low, until smooth.

7 Spread the chocolate mixture over the caramel while warm and leave to cool for 30 minutes. Cover with foil and chill for at least 30 minutes to set. To taste it at its best, take the shortbread out of the fridge 20 minutes before you eat it.

Lemon drizzle cake

Okay, maybe we're biased, but there's nothing quite as stunning as a well-made lemon drizzle cake. As always, it's a question of balance: the lemon flavour cuts through the sweetness of the cake beautifully. Serve it warm with a dollop of cream or crème fraîche as a pud, or slice it cold to nibble with tea.

Serves 8

110g butter, softened, plus extra to grease
110g caster sugar
140g self-raising flour
1 tsp baking powder
Zest of 1 lemon
2 medium eggs, beaten
2 tbsp milk

For the topping:
175g granulated sugar
Juice of 2 lemons

Prepare 15 minutes
Cook 35-40 minutes

1 Preheat the oven to 160°C/140°C fan oven/gas mark 2-3. Grease a 20cm x 10cm loaf tin with a little butter.

2 Put the butter into the bowl of a food processor and whiz with the sugar, flour, baking powder and lemon zest for approximately 30 seconds, or until all the ingredients are combined.

3 With the machine still running, slowly add the beaten eggs and then the milk until combined. The mix should be a smooth consistency, but not too firm and not too runny.

4 Spoon the mixture into the loaf tin and level the top with a spoon. Bake in the oven for 30-40 minutes. To check that the cake is cooked, insert a skewer or sharp knife into the middle. If it comes out clean the cake is cooked. If not, continue baking, but check every 5 minutes.

5 Take the lemon cake out of the loaf tin and place upside down on a cooling rack, resting on top of a lipped baking sheet. After 10 minutes, use a knife to pierce several holes over the top of the cake and pour half of the syrup all over. After 5 minutes or so, pour the rest of the sugar syrup over the lemon cake. This cake is best left for half an hour before eating, to allow the syrup to soak through. Store in an airtight container in a cool, dry place.

"If the cake is too hot when you're adding the lemon syrup, it will tend to run straight through, so let it cool down for about 10 minutes."

Eleni's tip

Doughnuts

Americans claim that the doughnut originated in the States; the Dutch claim that they invented it. Who knows the truth of the matter? Either way, its soft, pillowy sweetness when freshly made makes it impossible to resist.

Makes 30

15g dried yeast
450g strong bread flour
7g salt
45g caster sugar, plus extra for rolling
1 small egg
45g butter, melted
Vegetable or sunflower oil, for frying
Lemon curd, for the filling

Prepare 1 hour
Cook 10 minutes (or until golden)

1 Put the yeast in a bowl and add 200ml lukewarm water. Stir to mix and set aside for 10 minutes to dissolve completely.

2 Put the flour, salt, sugar and egg in the bowl of an electric mixer fitted with a dough hook. Add the butter and the yeast mixture. Knead for 10 minutes to make a smooth, elastic dough, adding an extra 30ml water if it looks dry. You can also do this stage by hand – the dough should be sticky, but not stick to your fingers.

3 Cover the bowl and set aside to rise for 1 hour until it feels springy. Divide into 30 pieces, then roll into balls. Put on a lightly floured board and prove until doubled in size.

4 Heat the oil in a deep-fat fryer or saucepan to 180°C (it's hot enough when a test ball sizzles). Fry the balls in batches until golden. Lift out and drain on kitchen paper to remove excess grease.

5 Put a couple of tablespoons caster sugar on to a plate and roll the warm doughnuts in the sugar to coat. Push a small sharp knife into the side of each doughnut and spoon (or pipe) a little lemon curd into each. Enjoy them fresh!

"This is a golden opportunity to use up any leftover jams or conserves. Also, a pinch of cinnamon in your rolling sugar is a nice touch." **James C's tip**

Gluten-free peanut butter cookies

How lucky we are that the smart 19th century American botanist, Dr George Washington Carver, saw the potential in turning the peanut into a cash crop. It was he who also came up with the genius idea of making biscuits with them. The fact that they're made with rice flour (which will please anyone with a gluten allergy), as well as delivering a huge protein punch, surely makes a virtue of devouring them?

Makes 10

65g unsalted butter
90g soft brown sugar
65g crunchy peanut butter
1 small egg, beaten
90g rice flour
½ tsp baking powder
½ tsp vanilla extract

Prepare 15 minutes
Cook 16-18 minutes

1 Preheat the oven to 180°C/160°C fan oven/gas mark 4 and lightly grease a baking tray.

2 In a bowl cream together the butter and sugar until light and fluffy. Beat in the peanut butter and egg, followed by the rice flour, baking powder and vanilla extract to make a soft dough.

3 Using a dessertspoon, place 10 evenly spaced mounds of dough on the baking tray.

4 Bake until just golden, but still soft. Remove from the oven and leave to cool for 2-3 minutes on the tray before carefully removing and cooling completely on a wire rack.

Raspberry & pistachio macaroons

Macaroons? Need I say more? This makes 20, but trust me, they'll go in the blink of an eye, so make as many as you can fit in the oven.

Makes 20

For the Italian meringue:
185g caster sugar
1 tsp green food colouring
2 medium egg whites (retain 1 yolk to use in the buttercream)

For the paste:
185g ground almonds
185g icing sugar
2 medium egg whites

For the raspberry buttercream:
90g raspberry coulis (store-bought)
1 medium egg yolk (saved from one of the egg whites above)
30g caster sugar
150g unsalted butter, diced

To garnish:
50g shelled, peeled pistachios

Prepare 90 minutes
Cook 12-15 minutes

1 Preheat the oven to 160°C/140°C fan oven/gas mark 2-3.

2 First make the Italian meringue: in a small saucepan, add the sugar to 75ml water and stir until there are no lumps. Add the green food colouring and stir the edge of the pan with a pastry brush dipped in cold water to wash down any grains of sugar clinging to the side and ensure there are no crystals remaining. Place the saucepan over a medium to high heat and use a sugar thermometer to check the temperature – it needs to reach 114°C.

3 Put the egg whites into an electric mixer bowl with the whisk attached and set aside, ready for when the sugar syrup has reached the required temperature.

4 Cut two sheets of parchment paper the same size as the baking trays and set aside ready for piping. Then place a 6mm nozzle in a piping bag and set aside.

5 Meanwhile, chop the pistachios and set aside.

6 Put the ground almonds and icing sugar into a medium-sized mixing bowl.

7 Continue to check the temperature of the sugar syrup: once it has reached 112°C, start whisking the egg whites on slow speed. When the temperature gets to 114°C, lift the thermometer out and slowly pour the syrup down the side of the electric mixer bowl, making sure you don't splash yourself. Turn to full speed. After about 5 minutes, the Italian meringue will become glossy and soft.

8 To make the paste, add the egg whites to the icing sugar and ground almond mixture and mix with a spatula until you have a paste. Once the Italian meringue starts forming soft peaks, combine it with the paste in two stages. If it is over-mixed, it will become too liquid and the macaroons will be very flat once they're cooked, so it's important to use a gentle mixing motion.

9 The macaroon mixture is now ready to be piped. With a spatula, half-fill the piping bag. Pipe some of the mixture on to each corner of the baking trays in order to anchor the parchment paper to the tray. Pipe in straight lines from left to right, leaving a 2cm gap in between each macaroon for expansion. Once both trays are full, sprinkle with the chopped pistachios before cooking.

10 Bake for 12 minutes – you'll know they're baked when you can lift them off the paper without leaving much residue. Once cooked, remove the trays from the oven and allow the macaroons to cool on the tray.

11 To make the raspberry buttercream, heat up the raspberry coulis over a medium heat.

12 In a separate bowl, whisk the egg yolk and sugar together.

13 Once the coulis begins to boil, add some to the egg mixture and combine with a spatula. Then transfer it to the saucepan with the rest of the coulis. Continue to stir over a low heat and, once the mixture coats the back of the spatula, pour it into the bowl of the electric mixer fitted with the paddle attachment. Mix on medium to high speed.

14 When the mixture has almost cooled in the electric mixer, add a third of the diced butter on low speed. After a minute, increase the speed and leave it for a further 3 minutes, then add another third of the diced butter, and repeat this process until all the butter has been added. The buttercream should become thick, smooth and shiny.

15 Using a spatula, spoon the mix into a piping bag. Pipe a small blob on to one macaroon and top with another, then do the same with the remaining macaroons until they've all been sandwiched.

Mushroom brioche

The word 'duxelle' is the culinary term used to describe minced button mushrooms, shallots and onions sautéed in butter and cooked until the liquid has evaporated. It was invented either in the village of Uzel in Brittany, or by Monsieur La Varenne, the chef who ran the kitchens belonging to the Marquis of Uxelles - whichever you prefer! Either way, it makes a delicious filling for delicate, buttery brioches.

Makes 12 rolls

For the mushroom duxelle:
35g unsalted butter
300g button mushrooms, finely chopped
1 banana shallot, finely chopped
50ml white wine

For the brioche:
7g dried yeast
85ml whole milk, warmed
360g strong flour
50g caster sugar
5g salt
2 large eggs
85g unsalted butter, diced and at room temperature

Prepare 40 minutes, plus rising and proving
Cook 10-12 minutes

1 For the duxelle, melt the butter in a frying pan or saucepan and fry the mushrooms and shallot until all the moisture is cooked out of the mixture. Add the white wine and continue to cook until all the liquid has evaporated.

2 Put the yeast in a small bowl and add the milk. Stir to mix together and set aside for 10 minutes to dissolve completely. Place the flour, sugar and salt together in the bowl of an electric mixer fitted with a dough hook. Crack the eggs into the flour mix, add the yeast mixture and, using the dough hook attachment, knead for 10 minutes until the dough is elastic. Gradually add the butter piece by piece until it is incorporated and you have a smooth and elastic dough. Cover and leave in a warm place for 1 hour to rise.

3 Take the proved dough and push it down with your hand to squeeze out the air. Roll out to a rectangular shape roughly 3mm thick, then pop in the freezer for 15 minutes (freezing the dough will allow you to work with it). Remove from the freezer and, using a palette knife, spread the duxelle mixture over the length of the dough, leaving an empty end without any mixture on it (you'll use this bit to seal it eventually). Then roll the dough up like a roulade and brush the empty end with a little water and seal. Cut into 12 slices and lie them flat on a baking tray, leaving space around each. Prove in a warm place for around 1 hour.

4 Half an hour before the end of proving time, preheat the oven to 180°C/160°C fan oven/gas mark 4 and bake for 10-12 minutes.

Flapjacks

Believe it or not, Shakespeare referred to flapjacks in 'Pericles, Prince of Tyre' ('...we'll have flesh for holidays, fish for fasting days, and moreo'er puddings and flap-jacks...'!). But it was only around 1935 that it became the oats-based version that we know and love today.

Makes 15

170g unsalted butter, plus extra to grease
85g soft brown sugar
85g golden syrup
35g honey
255g porridge oats
50g sultanas

Prepare 15 minutes
Cook 20-25 minutes

1 Preheat the oven to 200°C/180°C fan oven/gas mark 6. Grease and line a baking tin roughly 20cm x 15cm with baking parchment.

2 Put the butter in a medium pan and add the sugar, golden syrup and honey. Heat gently to melt the butter and continue to cook, stirring occasionally, until the sugar has dissolved.

3 Pour in the oats and sultanas and stir everything together thoroughly until the mixture is well combined. Spoon into the prepared tin and flatten the top with the back of a metal spoon.

4 Bake in the oven for 20-25 minutes until golden brown and bubbling at the edges.

5 Leave the flapjack in the tin to cool completely, then transfer to a board and cut into equal rectangles and serve.

6 Store in an airtight container in a cool, dry place and enjoy within 3 days.

"When lining the baking tin, line the sides too, to make it easier to take the flapjack out of the tin before cutting it. A bread knife is the easiest way to cut it."

James C's tip

Dark chocolate & peppermint truffles

These are delicious served with the Hot Chocolate with Hazelnut Cream on page 244.

Makes about 10

150g Lindt Dark Mint Chocolate (70% cocoa solids), chopped finely, plus 50g for rolling
120ml double cream
40g cocoa powder, for rolling

Prepare 40 minutes, plus 1 hour setting
Cook 5 minutes

1 Place the chocolate in a bowl. Boil the cream in a small pan and allow to stand for 30 seconds, then add to the chocolate.

2 Gradually stir the mixture, combining the two ingredients to make a ganache (chef-speak for the chocolate mixture), then set aside to cool. Once cooled, transfer to the fridge and allow to set for 1 hour.

3 Remove from the fridge and, using a teaspoon or a melon baller, scoop out a teaspoonful and shape into small balls. Transfer these to the freezer to set completely.

4 Melt the extra 50g chocolate in a bowl placed on top of a small pan of simmering water, making sure the base doesn't touch the water. With your fingertips, scoop out a small amount of the chocolate and put it in your palm. Roll each truffle in the melted chocolate and drop gently into the cocoa powder to coat. Refrigerate until ready to serve, then remove the truffles from the fridge 10 minutes before you eat them to let the flavours come through.

"If the mixture looks as though it's starting to separate as you're stirring the chocolate and cream together, correct by whisking in 1 tbsp of warm water or warm cream" **James C's tip**

Focaccia

This flatbread could well be an early version of pizza. After all, it would have been cooked on the hearth in front of a hot fire, which isn't a million miles away from the concept of the pizza oven. Different regions in Italy have their own take on focaccia, but essentially it's an olive oil bread to which you can add whatever you fancy: olives, garlic, herbs, cheese, onion, sundried tomatoes – anything goes.

Makes 1-2 loaves

1 head garlic
Small bunch rosemary
200ml olive oil
15g dried yeast
1kg strong white flour
580ml warm water
15g table salt
10g sea salt, to garnish

Prepare 30 minutes, plus around 4 hours rising and proving
Cook 25-30 minutes

1 Peel the garlic and place in a medium pan with half of the rosemary and the olive oil. Bring to just below boiling point then remove the pan from the heat and leave to infuse for about 20 minutes.

2 Put the yeast into the bowl of an electric mixer fitted with a dough hook and add 280ml of the warm water. Leave for 10 minutes to dissolve, then add the flour, the remaining water and the table salt.

3 Remove the spines from the remaining rosemary and chop them finely. Add to the bread dough with 40ml of the infused oil and knead in the electric mixer for about 10 minutes until the dough is nice and elastic. Return the dough to a bowl and cover with about 60ml infused oil. Set aside to rise for 2 hours in a warm place.

4 Grease two 30cm round ovenproof dishes or baking trays, or one 20cm x 30cm rectangular tin, with a little infused oil. Knock back the risen dough on a board, then roll out to the required shape before transferring to the prepared dishes or trays. Set aside to prove again for 45 minutes to 1 hour.

5 Drain the infused oil, then dimple the loaf with your fingers. Stud the dimples with rosemary sprigs and the garlic cloves from the oil, and set aside to prove again for 1 hour. Preheat the oven to 200°C/180°C fan oven/gas mark 6. Rub some infused oil over the top and sprinkle with sea salt, then bake for 25-30 minutes. Remove from the tin and cool on a wire rack.

6 Use the leftover oil and a little balsamic vinegar for dipping when eating the bread.

Bitter chocolate & sea salt caramel macaroons

This is a super-indulgent treat, but they're quite small, so they're worth it in moderation every now again when you're pushing the boat out. Besides, you have to live a little, too, right?

Makes 15-20 (depending on the size to which you pipe them)

For the Italian meringue:
185g caster sugar
2 medium egg whites

For the paste:
2 medium egg whites
185g icing sugar
165g ground almonds
25g cocoa powder

For the sea salt caramel:
25g liquid glucose
150g sugar
125ml whipping cream
15g unsalted butter
½ tsp sea salt

For the chocolate ganache:
200g dark chocolate (at least 70% cocoa solids), chopped finely
160g double cream

Prepare 90 minutes
Cook 12-15 minutes

1 Preheat the oven to 160°C/140°C fan oven/gas mark 3.

2 To make the Italian meringue, put the caster sugar and 75ml water in a small saucepan and mix until there are no lumps. Place the saucepan over medium to high heat and use a sugar thermometer to check the temperature - you're looking for 114°C.

3 In an electric mixing bowl, beat the 2 egg whites with the whisk attachment so that they're ready to use when the sugar syrup has reached the required temperature.

4 Cut out two sheets of parchment paper to the same size as your two baking trays and set aside ready for piping. Place an 8mm nozzle in a piping bag and set aside.

5 Once the sugar syrup has reached 114°C, lift the thermometer out and slowly pour the syrup down the side of the bowl of beaten egg whites (be careful not to splash yourself). Turn to full speed, and after about 5 minutes the Italian meringue will become glossy and soft. When soft peaks have formed, the meringue is ready.

6 To make the paste, add the 2 egg whites to the icing sugar, ground almonds and cocoa powder and combine with a spatula until a paste has formed.

7 Add the Italian meringue to the paste in two stages: if you over-mix, it will become too liquid and the macaroons will be very flat once they're cooked, so use a gentle mixing motion.

8 The macaroon mix is now ready to be piped. Using a spatula, half-fill the piping bag with the nozzle. Pipe some of the mixture into each corner of the baking trays in order to make the parchment paper stick to them. Pipe blobs in straight lines from left to right, leaving a 2cm gap in between each macaroon for expansion.

9 Bake for 12 minutes - they are baked when you can lift them off the paper without leaving much residue. Once cooked, remove the trays from the oven and leave the macaroons to cool on the trays.

10 To make the sea salt caramel, put the glucose in a heavy-based pan, place it over a medium heat and warm for 1-2 minutes. Gradually add the sugar and cook, stirring occasionally, until the mixture turns a rich caramel colour.

11 In a separate saucepan warm the cream. (This is important - if the cream is added straight from the fridge, the caramel will react by bubbling vigorously, which can be very dangerous.) Then, dice the butter.

12 Add the warm cream, diced butter and sea salt to the sugar mixture. Once all the lumps have disappeared and the caramel is a smooth consistency, pour into a tray and allow to cool.

13 To make the chocolate ganache, place the chocolate in a bowl. Pour the cream into a pan and bring it to the boil, then pour it over the chocolate. Stir gently to combine and set aside to cool.

14 Once cool, mix with the desired amount of sea salt caramel to suit your taste and spoon the mixture into a piping bag fitted with a 4mm round piping nozzle. Pipe a small blob on to one macaroon and top with another, then do the same with the remaining macaroons until they've all been sandwiched.

"Make sure you cook the caramel until it's a rich hazelnut brown." **James C's tip**

Flourless chocolate cakes with Chantilly cream

The great joy of these cakes is their texture, but also the fact that even people who have a gluten allergy can enjoy their delicious moistness. Saturated with rich, dark chocolate and with ground almonds to hold the moisture in, it's more of a dessert than a cake for afternoon tea - although, of course, it's great any time. Pure, wicked indulgence. Bring it on!

Serves 4

For the chocolate cake:
225g dark chocolate (70% cocoa solids)
100g unsalted butter
100g caster sugar
3 medium eggs, separated
25g ground almonds
Salt

For the Chantilly cream:
200ml whipping cream
30g icing sugar
Seeds from 1 vanilla pod

For the chocolate sauce:
150ml whipping cream
75g dark chocolate (70% cocoa solids)
25g milk chocolate

Icing sugar, to dust

Prepare 20 minutes
Cook 10 minutes

1 Preheat the oven to 180°C/160°C fan oven/gas mark 4. Melt the chocolate in a bowl resting over a pan of simmering water, making sure the base doesn't touch the water. Then let it cool a little. In a separate bowl beat together the butter and sugar for around 10 minutes until the mixture is light and fluffy in texture.

2 Beat in the egg yolks quickly, then fold in the melted chocolate and the ground almonds.

3 In a separate bowl, whisk the egg whites in a clean, grease-free bowl until trebled in volume, then add a pinch of salt. Continue to whisk until the mixture stands in soft peaks. Fold a large spoonful through the chocolate mixture, then continue to fold in the remainder very carefully in two more stages. Divide the mix between four greased moulds (a 10-12cm flan mould is the most suitable here). Fill the mould to about two-thirds of the way up and bake in the oven for 10 minutes or until the cake feels firm to the touch. The cake will rise beautifully, but will collapse slightly after cooling - this is quite normal. Set aside to cool slightly.

4 To make the Chantilly cream, whisk all the ingredients together in a bowl until firm, then chill.

5 To make the chocolate sauce, bring the cream to the boil in a pan. Remove from the heat and whisk in both types of chocolate until melted. Set aside.

6 To assemble, unmould each cake - they should still be slightly warm - and spoon a little Chantilly cream on the side. Drizzle a little chocolate sauce around the plate for a decorative touch and sprinkle a light dusting of icing sugar over each cake.

Glossary

Anchovies
Anchovies are small, blue-green fish with a silver stripe. They vary from 2cm to 40cm in adult length, and are sold layered with salt, as whole fish in oil, as fillets in cans, or packed in jars.

Bamboo shoots
The shoots of the bamboo are cut when they have grown to around 15cm (6in) above the ground. Used as an ingredient, they need to be peeled and the inner white part boiled for 30 minutes in water. However, the canned variety requires boiling for only 10 minutes and can be used immediately in soups or curries. Canned bamboo shoots can be refrigerated if the water is renewed daily.

Basil (Holy)
Hindus believe that basil is sacred, and they like to plant it in religious sanctuaries. The variety of basil they use is called 'holy basil', and it has a spicy flavour. This is more difficult to find in the West than sweet basil, but pepper or finely chopped chilli can be added to the sweet variety to mimic the flavour. Both types are used extensively in Thai cooking.

Bean curd
This is a soya bean extract to which a setting agent has been added. Soft bean curd is white and is used widely in Chinese dishes. It comes in many forms (fried and fermented are two common examples) and is available in most oriental shops, usually sold in 7.5cm (3 in) cubes. Hard or dry bean curd is made by compressing soft bean curd.

Bergamot
This is a small, yellow, sour citrus fruit similar to the orange and usually cultivated in Calabria (Italy). The rind contains an essential oil used in perfumery, confectionery and, also, Earl Grey tea.

Bruschetta
Originally from Italy, bruschetta is a slice of bread that is grilled on both sides and eaten warm with olive oil and garlic.

Capers
These are flower buds which come from a shrub that is native to eastern Asia, but can also be found in other hot regions. They are used either as a condiment, pickled in vinegar, preserved in brine, or in dry, coarse salt. They are used to flavour dishes such as rice and meatballs, and to garnish pizzas - they also go well with mustard and horseradish.

Chinese mushrooms
Also called shiitake mushrooms, these are the most widely used mushrooms in oriental cooking. They are grown in China and Japan on the wood of dead deciduous trees: the spawn is planted in wedges cut into logs, and the crops last for three to six years. Shiitake are either dried in the sun or via artificial heat - the dried variety need to be soaked in warm water for 20 minutes before use.

Chorizo
This is a Spanish sausage flavoured with red peppers, and it can be smoked or plain. As a cooking ingredient, it is best when flavoured with garlic. Chorizo can also be cured - eaten this way, it is sliced thinly and served as tapas on bread.

Coconut cream
Coconut cream is very similar to coconut milk, but contains less water. The difference is mainly in the consistency: it is thicker and more paste-like, while coconut milk is generally a liquid.

Coconut milk
Coconut milk is a sweet, milky, white cooking base derived from the meat of a mature coconut. The colour and rich taste of the milk can be attributed to the high oil content and sugars. It provides the base of many Indonesian, Malaysian and Thai curries.

Coriander
Native to southern Europe and the Middle East, this herb is now available worldwide. Both the fresh leaves and the seeds are used. Coriander has a fresh taste that is similar to orange, and it is an important ingredient in curry.

Cornmeal
Cornmeal is flour ground from dried maize or American corn. It is a common staple food and can be ground to fine, medium or coarse consistencies. In the United States, finely ground cornmeal is also referred to as 'cornflour'. However, in British recipes the word 'cornflour' denotes cornstarch.

Crème fraîche
This is a cream to which a lactic bacteria culture has been added, which thickens it and imparts a slightly sharp, but not sour, flavour. It is thicker and sweeter than sour cream, contains 12-15% fat, and needs to be consumed within 48 hours of opening. Originally a French product, it is now widely available in many countries.

Garlic
The famously powerful, pungent bulb is covered in a papery skin that can be white, pink or purple tinged. New season or wet garlic has a milder, sweeter flavour than the drier bulbs. Mostly used as a spice or an aromatic, raw garlic can be added to flavour dressings and butters, or fried at the beginning of savoury recipes.

Ham, Iberico and Serrano
The Spanish adore ham, which is no surprise, since they produce some of the best in the world. Serrano ham is cured, and is excellent as an ingredient in cooking. Iberico ham is considered to be one of Spain's finest, and comes from pigs that have been allowed to roam free in the oak forests, enjoying plenty of exercise and feeding on acorns. The finest hams, such as Iberico, are best saved for enjoying with a glass of chilled Manzanilla sherry, so that you can savour their distinctive flavour.

Kaffir lime leaves
These impart an intense floral and citrus flavour, and are almost always required in Thai curries. Lime zest, while not the same, will give the dish a similarly refreshing citrus flavour.

Meze
This is a plentiful assortment of small plates of simple food traditionally found in Greece, Turkey and the Middle East. Either served as party snacks for a large group, a meal in their own right, or a starter course for a large-scale event, they include olives, taramasalata, cold meats, dips, salads and pitta bread.

Okra (or ladies' fingers)
This is a vegetable that people either love or hate, due to its slimy texture. To avoid this, okra pods are often briefly stir-fried or cooked with acidic ingredients such as citrus, tomatoes or vinegar. A few drops of lemon juice will usually suffice. They are very popular in the Caribbean, India and Greece. In Indian cooking they are known as 'bhindi' and are added to curries or bhajis. If they give a nice snap, they are fresh, but if they are bendy, it means they're old, stale and not worth buying.

Olive oil
There are two main grades of olive oil: extra virgin olive oil and olive oil. Extra virgin olive oil is unique among cooking oils: made directly from the fresh juice of the olive, it is then pickled, milled and pressed, and the resulting juice separated into oil and water. If the oil meets the required standard, it is bottled and sold as extra virgin olive oil. If it fails the taste and chemical requirements for extra virgin status, it is refined and bottled as olive oil. Extra virgin olive oil has less than 1% acidity. Ordinary olive oil has about 15% extra virgin olive oil added to it to give it a milder flavour. Ordinary olive oil is best used in high-temperature cooking and deep-frying, as it has a high smoke point. Extra virgin olive oil has a lower smoke point but will stand up to flash-frying, grilling, basting and pot-roasting.

Paella
This is a traditional Spanish rice dish garnished with vegetables, chicken and shellfish. Its name is derived from that of the large, round, shallow and open pan with handles in which it is prepared, called a 'paellera'. Its three basic ingredients are rice, saffron and olive oil.

Pasta
Pasta is categorised in two basic styles: dried and fresh. Dried pasta made without eggs can be stored for up to two years under ideal conditions, while fresh pasta will keep for a few days when refrigerated. (Surprisingly, the Italians do not use fresh pasta as much as dried.) There are two premium brands - although supermarket pasta is perfectly acceptable, look out for De Cecco, which comes in a turquoise blue packet, or Voiello, which is made in Parma, Italy. Pasta should be cooked in salted, boiling water, keeping strictly to the recommended cooking time so that it is served al dente.

Pepper
Peppercorns are the berries of a tropical vine. They can be black, white or green, depending on how mature they were when they were harvested.

Black peppercorns These are the most pungent, and must be crushed or ground.

Green peppercorns These are unripe black peppercorns - they have the mildest flavour and are usually used whole or crushed.

Pink peppercorns These aren't actually a peppercorn at all, but the mild-flavoured berry of a South American plant. They are sometimes included in peppercorn mixtures, and are a popular seasoning for fish. However, they can cause adverse effects, so should be used sparingly.

Sichuan pepper These aromatic, reddish-brown berries, also known as anise pepper, resemble peppercorns but come from a completely different plant. The pungent, mouth-tingling, slightly citrus flavour is popular in Chinese cooking and goes well with duck and chicken. It is also an essential component of Chinese five-spice powder.

White peppercorns These are the fully ripe berries that have had the outer skin removed. They retain the heat of black pepper, but are less fragrant.

Polenta
Polenta is a cornmeal porridge and is the traditional, basic dish of northern Italy, available both finely and coarsely ground. It is traditionally made with water in a large copper pot and used to accompany fish, game and meat dishes.

Porcini mushrooms, dried
Drying mushrooms concentrates their flavour - they are almost more valuable dried than they are fresh. They need to be reconstituted in water before they are used, and you should save the liquid for stocks and sauces, because it has great flavour. Just discard the last couple of teaspoonfuls, which is often quite gritty.

Salt
Crystal rock salt Obtained from underground deposits, crystal salt is less refined than table salt.

Sea salt Sea salt is said to be the best salt of all - the crystals are obtained via the evaporation of sea water.

Table salt This is rock salt obtained from underground deposits. It is usually refined and treated with magnesium carbonate to prevent caking and help it pour more easily.

Water chestnut
There are two types of water chestnut. Trapa natans has an edible seed and a floury texture, and is eaten raw, roasted or boiled all over Central Europe and Asia. A related aquatic plant, Trapa bicornis, is grown in China, Korea and Japan. Its seeds are eaten boiled or preserved in honey and sugar, or are used for making flour. The Chinese water chestnut, or 'pi tsi', is a tuber that is cultivated in the East Indies, China and Japan. It is usually used as a vegetable, and outside of Asia is normally bought canned.

NOODLES
Flat rice noodles
These can be found in some of the larger supermarkets, but are mainly stocked by Asian grocers. They are very delicate and break easily. They should be soaked in cold water for about an hour, and can then be dipped in hot water for 2-3 seconds. They are usually added to dishes such as pad Thai noodles, and are cooked with the other ingredients for a minute or two until tender and heated through.

Medium egg noodles
Chinese egg noodles are basically eggs and flour, just like pasta. Contrary to the instructions on the packet, they are best dropped into a pan of boiling water, brought back to the boil and then removed from the heat and left to soak for 4 minutes. This way they will retain a bit of bite, rather than becoming soggy.

Vermicelli noodles
Rice vermicelli are found in several Asian dishes, where they are often eaten as part of a soup dish, stir-fry or salad. They are also sold dried, and must be soaked before using, but be careful not to over-soak them, as they will stick together and form a lump. Just drop them into a pan of boiling water, then remove from the heat and leave them for a further minute. Use straightaway to prevent them from sticking together.

RICE
Basmati rice
This is a variety of long-grain rice grown in India and Pakistan, notable for its fragrance and delicate flavour. It should first be picked over for small stones, then rinsed in cold water to remove the excess starch. It swells up to three times its length and has a wonderful fragrance during cooking.

Risotto rice
Risotto is a traditional Italian rice dish cooked with broth and flavoured with Parmesan cheese and other ingredients, which can include meat, fish or vegetables. The name literally means 'little rice', and it is one of the most common ways of cooking rice in Italy. This short-grain variety of rice is essential for making risotto, because the outside of the grain breaks down during cooking and thickens the liquid, while the centre retains some bite and gives the finished dish its classic creamy texture.

Thai jasmine rice
This is a jasmine-scented rice from Thailand. It is similar in appearance to basmati rice and tends to cling together in small lumps during cooking. It is the perfect accompaniment to all Thai and Far Eastern dishes.

SAUCES
Chilli sauce
This is a popular ingredient in many cuisines such as Indian, Mexican and Jamaican. It is very similar to sweet chilli sauce, but lacks the sugar. Some versions have garlic and ginger added to them.

Dark soy sauce
We are all familiar with soy sauce, which is made from fermented and salted soya beans, but it is important to know which one to buy. The best brand to opt for is the Japanese variety called 'Kikkoman', which is richer and has a deeper, slightly sweeter flavour than the others.

Ketchup manis
This is a sweet soy sauce that has a thick, almost syrupy consistency and a pronounced sweet, treacle-like flavour owing to the generous addition of palm sugar. It is a unique variety that, at a pinch, can be replaced with molasses with a little vegetable stock stirred in.

Light soy sauce
Lighter in colour, thinner and much saltier than dark soy sauce, this is normally used when the recipe requires the colour of a dish to remain unchanged.

Sweet chilli sauce
This chilli sauce is made with chillies, sugar, vinegar and salt. There are a number of makes on the market, but by far the best is Lingham's Chilli Sauce. Made from 100% fresh chillies, it contains no preservatives and no tomato paste or purée.

Thai fish sauce
Also called 'nam pla' in Thailand, this condiment derives from fermented fish, and is an essential ingredient in many curries and sauces. Thai fish sauce is often made from anchovies, salt and water, and tends to be used in moderation due to its intense flavour. One of the most popular is Squid Brand, which comes in large bottles. Make ensure you buy one that has a light, clear colour - if the liquid is dark, it will be old and overly fishy.

SEEDS
Fennel seeds
These have a sweet aniseed flavour and go exceptionally well with fish and meat. They are available in supermarkets that offer a good selection of spices.

Fenugreek seeds
Fenugreek seeds are frequently a component in pickles, curry powders and pastes, and the spice is often found in Indian cuisine. They are used as seasoning in many dishes or in powdered form to mix with rice.

Mustard seeds
Black mustard seeds lose their heat and take on a nutty flavour when lightly fried in hot oil. They tend to be used in some Indian curries and salads. Yellow mustard seeds, apart from being the main ingredient of mustard, are one of a number of spices used to make American 'shrimp boil seasoning', and add a pleasing heat to the dish.

Sesame oil
Sesame oil (also known as gingelly oil or til oil) is an edible vegetable oil derived from sesame seeds. Besides being used as cooking oil in south India,

it is often used as a flavour enhancer in Chinese, Korean and, to a lesser extent, Southeast Asian cuisine. The cold-pressed oil is light, delicate and ideal for dishes where you don't want the flavour of oil to dominate. Roasted sesame oil, pressed from toasted sesame seeds, is much stronger and should be used sparingly.

Star anise
This is the dried, star-shaped fruit of an evergreen tree that is native to China. The seeds are contained in pods.

White poppy seeds
These small, creamy-white seeds are usually ground to a powder and used to thicken curry sauces. They add a nutty flavour, especially if lightly roasted first. A good alternative is ground almonds.

SPICES
Asafoetida
Asafoetida has a pungent, unpleasant smell when raw, but in cooked dishes delivers a smooth flavour reminiscent of leeks. It is widely available in India, where is used as a digestive aid, a condiment, and an ingredient in pickles. Its odour, when uncooked, is so strong that it must be stored in an airtight container, otherwise it will contaminate other spices in its vicinity. However, the odour and flavour become much milder and more pleasant when heated in oil.

Blachan (dried shrimp paste)
Shrimp paste or shrimp sauce is a common ingredient used in Southeast Asian and southern Chinese cuisine. It is made from fermented ground shrimp, which is sundried and cut into fist-sized rectangular blocks. It is not designed, or customarily used, for immediate consumption, and has to be fully cooked before being eaten.

Cardamom
The queen of spices, cardamom has been used since ancient times. Produced mostly in India and Sri Lanka, it also grows in Southeast Thailand near Cambodia. The aromatic pods can be green, white or black and they all contain a number of small seeds. The pods and seeds are used in different types of sweet and savoury Thai dishes, especially curries.

Cayenne pepper
Made from the tiny cayenne chilli, this fine, brownish-red chilli powder is extremely hot. It is most often used as a seasoning to flavour mild and creamy sauces, egg dishes and stews. Cayenne pepper can also be used to spice up savoury biscuits such as cheese straws, or boost barbecue sauces and marinades.

Chinese five-spice powder
Used in Chinese cuisine for a variety of savoury dishes, this is a blend of spices consisting of anise pepper, star anise, cassia, cloves and fennel seed, with a dominant liquorice flavour. Available in powder form.

Cinnamon
This is the dried, aromatic bark of an evergreen belonging to the laurel family, and is native to Sri Lanka and India. Cinnamon is used in the form of quills, bark and powder, and has great keeping qualities. It is usually used in baking and desserts, but can also add flavour to rice, fish, chicken or ham dishes. Another variety of cinnamon, known as cassia, is best suited to spiced meats and curries.

Cloves
These are the dried, aromatic flower buds of an evergreen member of the myrtle family, native to Southeast Asia. Cloves are normally used whole, but the central 'head' of the bud can also be ground into a powder. They are used in sweet and savoury dishes, spiced wines and liqueurs.

Curry leaves
These leaves are highly valued (especially in curries) as seasoning in southern and west-coast Indian cooking, much like bay leaves. They are usually fried, along with chopped onion, in the first stage of preparation. In their fresh form, they have a short shelf life and don't keep well in the fridge. They are also available dried, though the aroma is largely inferior.

Curry paste
This is a moist blend of ground or pounded herbs and/or spices and other seasonings. Curry paste is primarily known as an important ingredient in Thai cuisine, and it can also be a generic commercial product that's a substitute for curry powder or spice blends used in other cuisines.

Galangal
This is a rhizome that is related to ginger and is available in most oriental food shops and some good supermarkets.

Ginger
Native to Southeast Asia, this spice comes from the rhizome of the plant. Its uses include baking, confectionery and liqueurs, as well as oriental dishes and pickles. Sold in root, powder and pickled forms.

Lemongrass
A native of Southeast Asia, lemongrass includes several species of grass, all possessing the flavour of grass and also of lemon, owing to the presence of citrus oils. It is useful for flavouring salads, fish dishes and soups, and is available in a powdered form known as Sereh Powder. In Thailand and other parts of Southeast Asia, the leaves of the kaffir lime are also used for fish dishes.

Paprika
This is a type of sweet red pepper that is dried and ground. Paprika is an earthy, terracotta-red powder and ranges from very mild to very hot. It is a key ingredient in Hungarian, Spanish and Austrian cooking.

Saffron
This spice is made from the dried stigmas of the saffron crocus, a bulbous plant originating in the East, introduced to Spain by the Arabs and later cultivated in the Mediterranean regions. Saffron is an intense yellow colour, with a pungent smell and bitter flavour. Commonly used in paella, risotto and Indian dishes, it is also found in some desserts, where it is used to flavour rice cooked in milk, semolina puddings and some types of brioche. Used in cooking, saffron is blended in hot liquid – it should never be fried quickly in very hot fat.

Tamarind
Cultivated in Asia for thousands of years, this pod-shaped fruit tastes either sweet or sour and is used in many Thai kitchens. The pulp is soaked for around 15 minutes in warm water and then squeezed, which loosens the 'meat' from the seeds and fibre. The juice is then drained off and used as per recipe instructions. In the West, it is famously used as as an ingredient in Worcestershire sauce.

Turmeric, ground
This bright yellow spice is ground from dried turmeric and has a musky, slightly bitter flavour. An essential ingredient in many Indian-style dishes, it is also popular in pickles such as piccalilli, chutneys and relishes. It is also used in some Southeast Asian cooking.

VINEGARS
Balsamic vinegar
This is a dark, smooth vinegar made only in and around Modena, north Italy. Aged in oak casks, the longer the ageing time, the better it gets and the more expensive it becomes. Use a younger, cheaper vinegar for cooking, and save the good, expensive stuff for dressing salads.

Coconut vinegar
Also known as 'coconut toddy' or 'palm vinegar', this is one of the most common vinegars used in Southeast Asia. Produced from the sap of the coconut palm, it is a milky colour with a mild, slightly fruity flavour. White wine vinegar is an adequate substitute.

Sherry vinegar
This is good in cooking, but its strong flavour makes it a little unpalatable in cold salad dressings. As with so many vinegars, there is much variation between the best and the worst. Vinagre de Jerez Gran Gusto is a favourite – Jerez is famous for its sherry and equally so for its vinegar.

White wine vinegar
This is important for salad dressings. Two popular vinegars are by Martin Pouret from Orleans and Menier from Bordeaux, both imported into this country. They are produced according to the Orleans method, which takes more time and uses good quality wine, making them more expensive, but well worth the cost. Wine is poured into barrels, some vinegar is added together with a vinegar culture, and the barrels are left open to the air, where the culture slowly turns the alcohol in the wine into vinegar. Cheap vinegar is made by mechanically oxygenating wine with a culture in a tank kept at blood temperature. This is a quicker process, but produces a harsher tasting vinegar that lacks subtle flavours.

Conversion charts

Points to keep in mind

All food is now sold in metric units, so it makes sense to measure ingredients that way, too.

Don't switch between metric and imperial in the same recipe. There are small discrepancies between equivalent weights, and you could end up with the wrong proportions of ingredients.

Invest in some electronic scales - they make it easy to weigh accurately in grams, or in ounces.

On tall, narrow measuring jugs there is a greater distance between the calibrations on the side, making it easier to judge small differences in quantities.

If making jam, the Guild of Food Writers recommends following the general rule of 500g sugar to 500ml fruit pulp (roughly 1 lb to 1 pint).

Unless otherwise stated, spoon measurements are level. These convert easily to millilitres, and vice versa - but remember, this applies to designated measuring spoons, whereas domestic cutlery may not correspond to the equivalents given below:

1 tablespoon = 15ml
1 dessertspoon = 10ml
1 teaspoon = 5ml

OVEN TEMPERATURES

Conventional oven	°C	°C fan oven	Gas
Very slow	140	120	1
Slow	150	130	2
Warm	170	150	3
Moderate	180	160	4
Moderate Hot	190	170	5
Fairly Hot	200	180	6
Hot	220	200	7
Very Hot	230	210	8
Extremely Hot	240	230	9

These conversions are approximate - they have either been rounded up or rounded down.

Butter used in cooking is unsalted, unless specified otherwise.

Eggs used are medium in size, unless otherwise stated.

DIMENSIONS

Imperial	Metric
⅛ inch	3 mm
¼ inch	5 mm
½ inch	1 cm
¾ inch	2 cm
1 inch	2.5 cm
1¼ inch	3 cm
1½ inch	4 cm
1¾ inch	4.5 cm
2 inch	5 cm
2½ inch	6 cm
3 inch	7.5 cm
3½ inch	9 cm
4 inch	10 cm
5 inch	13 cm
5¼ inch	13.5 cm
6 inch	15 cm
6½ inch	16 cm
7 inch	18 cm
7½ inch	19 cm
8 inch	20 cm
9 inch	23 cm
9½ inch	24 cm
10 inch	25.5 cm
11 inch	28 cm
12 inch	30 cm

WEIGHTS

Imperial	Metric
½ oz	10g
¾ oz	20g
1 oz	25g
1½ oz	40g
2 oz	50g
2½ oz	60g
3 oz	75g
4 oz	110g
4½ oz	125g
5 oz	150g
6 oz	175g
7 oz	200g
8 oz	225g
9 oz	250g
10 oz	275g
12 oz	350g
1 lb	450g
1 lb 8 oz	700g
2 lb	900g
3 lb	1.35kg

VOLUME

Imperial	Metric
2 fl oz	55 ml
3 fl oz	75 ml
5 fl oz (¼ pint)	150 ml
10 fl oz (½ pint)	275 ml
1 pint	570 ml
1 ¼ pint	725 ml
1 ¾ pint	1 litre
2 pint	1.2 litre
2½ pint	1.5 litre
4 pint	2.25 litres

Index

Acknowledgments

On behalf of the whole team at the Waitrose Cookery School, we would like to thank the following friends, family, equipment suppliers and partners for their dedicated help and generosity.

Waitrose Managing Director Mark Price, for his constant support, drive, vision and belief; nutritional expert and foodie friend Moira Howie; technologist Alison Gardner for her understanding and keeping us right; and wine buyer Anne Jones for her knowledge and expertise in pairing wines with recipes. Our very best neighbours Kevin Shipley, Paul Savill and all the partners at the John Barnes Store for being so patient with us in gathering ingredients, and for having the greatest store cupboard in the world to work with. Nathalie Heath and the press team; Sarah Fuller and the marketing team; and our ingredients suppliers, whose passion for their produce makes our efforts possible. Simon & Schuster editorial director Francine Lawrence; creative director Nigel Wright; photographer Ruth Jenkinson and assistant Carly Churchill; editor Hilary Ivory; and last but not least, home economist Emma Marsden.

Most importantly we would like to thank our equipment suppliers, whose generosity (as well as their great equipment and staff) helps inspire our customers when they cook. Amelia at All-Clad for the best pans and utensils on the market (we think, anyway); the whole Kenwood team for such a funky range of blenders and mixers; Le Creuset for their great quality and choice; George East for always being at the end of the phone when needed; Salter and their much-used scales; Joseph Joseph for their colourful and functional chopping boards; Oxo for their robust utensils; Riedel glassware, which adds a touch of class to our wine; Mermaid for solid, strong and reliable baking trays; and Robert Welch knives, which stay consistently sharp. And finally, a big thank-you to the John Lewis team for the provision of our stunning kitchens.